celebraTORI

G

gallery books

NEW YORK

LONDON

TORONTO

SYDNEY

NEW DELHI

celebra*TORI*

{ UNLEASHING YOUR INNER PARTY PLANNER

TO ENTERTAIN FRIENDS AND FAMILY }

TORI SPELLING

Gallery Books
A Division of Simon & Schuster, Inc.
1230 Avenue of the Americas
New York, NY 10020

First Gallery Books hardcover edition April 2012

GALLERY BOOKS and colophon are registered trademarks of Simon & Schuster, Inc.

For information about special discounts for bulk purchases, please contact Simon & Schuster Special Sales at 1-866-506-1949 or business@simonandschuster.com.

The Simon & Schuster Speakers Bureau can bring authors to your live event. For more information or to book an event contact the Simon & Schuster Speakers Bureau at 1-866-248-3049 or visit our website at www.simonspeakers.com.

Designed by Jaime Putorti

Manufactured in the United States of America

10 9 8 7 6 5 4 3 2 1

Library of Congress Cataloging-in-Publication data is available.

ISBN 978-1-4516-2790-9
ISBN 978-1-4516-2863-0 (ebook)

To my mom,

the master party planner.

I learned everything I know from watching you throw

the most amazing parties

with so much love. Thank you for the gift of knowing

it's all in the details.

I hope my parties make you proud!

I love you,

Tori xoxo

contents

introduction

a party planner is born

I come from a family that did everything over the top. We had the grandest house and the biggest parties. Whenever most people had one of something, we had five—from cars to bathrooms to dogs. I remember going to my parents' famous parties as a child. There was a Christmas party every year, where thousands of dollars must have been spent on the caviar alone. For one huge New Year's Eve bash my parents rented out the parking lot of the popular Beverly Hills restaurant Chasen's and tented it. The tent was elegantly swagged and, as I remember it, the entire lot was carpeted. I have no idea where people parked—I was young and blissfully free of such concerns—but there must have been a valet. There was a private patio at Chasen's that was often used for parties, but even as a kid I was aware that booking the whole parking lot on New Year's Eve was a big deal.

What made my mother's parties amazing (because, let's face it, my father was a little too busy making TV shows) were the grand florals, the gleaming silver trays, the exquisite food presentation, and elegant details like a piano player or a soloist. But spectacular as those parties were, party planning has evolved. The parties were extravagant, yes—the massive refilling bowls of caviar, a whole roast pig with an apple stuffed in its mouth—but they were simple in concept nonetheless.

My mother's parties have changed with the times, and these days she continues to set a high bar, embellishing her customary extravagance with amazing little touches that inspire me in my comparatively humble, do-it-yourself way. Take the spectacular candy table, which filled an entire room at her Christmas party. It had an electric train running full circle around it, through a village of colorful candy jars and confections artistically placed at

different heights. My mother's candy table was a catered masterpiece, and I can't exactly replicate the splendor of that creation. When I do a candy table, I do it myself, with store-bought candy and inexpensive canisters, but given the price difference I have to say it gives hers a run for the money.

CHILDHOOD PARTIES—EARLY INSPIRATION

Growing up, my birthday parties were always as over-the-top as the parties my parents threw for themselves and their friends. The celebrations that were thrown for me when I was little were the talk of the town. Usually in the backyard of our house in Beverly Hills, there were puppet shows and poodle shows, fair rides like bumper cars and twirling swings. We had McDonald's Happy Meals (a concession to my taste) and ice cream from Baskin-Robbins in all thirty-one flavors.

My eighth birthday party is the first one I really remember helping to plan. It was a roller-skating party, held in West Hollywood at a famous old rink called Flipper's Roller Boogie Palace. I designed my own outfit for the occasion: hot pink spandex pants and a turquoise tube top. Over the tube top I tied a pink-and-white top that said "Tori" on the back in rhinestone script. Linda Ronstadt, who had a similar look on her album, *Living in the USA,* would have been proud of me. The party was decorated with hot pink and turquoise balloons, streamers, and paper products. The cake, which was of course from Hansen's, *the* cake-makers of Hollywood, was custom-molded in the shape of a roller skate that looked just like mine, white with pink wheels. A caricature artist was there, drawing pictures of each guest engaged in his or her favorite activity. He rendered me, side view, sporting a gigantic roller skate. That party, which took place more than thirty years ago, was an unforgettable milestone for me: The first time I hosted a color-coordinated theme party. My very own color scheme at age eight. I was on my way to bigger and better things. In my not-too-distant future: a Michael Jackson party in fifth grade, with a Michael Jackson impersonator that my mother still insists was the King of Pop himself; a country club party in sixth grade; in seventh grade an all-girls spa party at the legendary Aida Grey beauty salon, where we got our makeup done and our hair blown out. Afterward we went to The Bistro Garden in Beverly Hills, which was Nancy Reagan's favorite restaurant before it was bought by Wolfgang Puck and made into Spago. As we sat on the patio and lunched, we were treated to a teen fashion show from Energy, which was my favorite boutique at the time.

When I was in sixth grade, my parents bought the property that they would transform into the Manor, a super mansion in Holmby Hills. Before they tore down Bing Crosby's mansion, they threw me a huge birthday party on the lawn. And the last birthday party I remember was my sixteenth, in tenth grade, which was a tea luncheon under a tent in the

backyard of our Beverly Hills house. In an effort to show my maturity, I wore a suit and had my hair in an updo. The tables were fancily set, as if it were a wedding, and at each place setting was an individual cake, as elaborate as a wedding cake, from the bakery Sweet Lady Jane. That was the birthday when I was given a champagne-colored BMW, when all I had hoped for was something a little less ostentatious and a little more fun.

BECOMING A HOST

I guess the celebrations of my youth planted a seed, either that or party planning was in my DNA, because as soon as I could, I started hosting my own parties. The first year I moved into my own apartment, my best friend Jenny and I decided to host Thanksgiving. We were nineteen years old, and we thought it was a very grown-up thing to cook a Thanksgiving feast. Of course, most of our friends were still locked into Thanksgiving with their families, so we set ours for Wednesday night, the day before the real holiday. (When you're nineteen, you don't see anything unappealing about stuffing your face two days in a row.)

I was still acting on *90210* at the time, and the day of the party, filming ran later than scheduled. I arrived home at five o'clock that night to find Jenny in the kitchen, sweat pouring down her face. The kitchen was a mess, with half-started dishes on every surface. Jenny said, "Why did we decide to do this?" She wiped her brow.

I said, "We can do it!"

Jenny said, "The chopped liver. It's over there." She pointed a wooden spoon in the direction of the liver, which I had insisted on making from scratch. We got to work, cooking and drinking and greeting guests as they arrived for dinner to find that it was hours from being ready.

At eleven o'clock that night, we were finally done. Jenny and I were excited to have our first real dinner on my new dining room table. But my then-boyfriend Nick and his friends were caught up in some sports game and refused to come in and eat at the table. So the girls ate at the table and the boys stayed in front of the television. The dishes didn't look spectacular, and everyone was so hungry it was hard to tell if the food was actually good, but we had succeeded.

(Before I served Nick his turkey, I put a few drops of Visine on it. I had heard it caused gastrointestinal distress. The special ingredient was meant to be payback not just for the TV watching during my dinner, but for all the nights he partied it up and left me at home. If he noticed a weird taste and complained, I was going to make that old fly-in-my-soup joke and tell him to be quiet, or everybody else would want what he got. As far as I know, the Visine didn't have the intended effect, but I was still somewhat vindicated. *Disclaimer: Don't try this at home.*)

That Thanksgiving Jenny and I had tried to cook every single recipe that struck our fancy. It was our first lesson in being overly ambitious. But for the most part we were undaunted by the chaos. Jenny and I continued to throw parties—all very experimental, spaghetti-on-the-wall type stuff. Literally. One of my friends always joked about how there was always old spaghetti hanging off the ceiling in that apartment. For every party we threw, Jenny and I would pick a gazillion recipes and cook all day long. There was no rhyme or reason to our labor. If we were hungry for deviled eggs, we made deviled eggs. If artichoke chicken sounded yummy, we threw it in. The only unifying theme for the menu was that it came from a pile of recipes we wanted to try. Although décor has become my obsession, I didn't care much about it at the time. But all that experimentation was fun, and it laid a good foundation for future parties. By the time I wanted to do a spooky Halloween spread, I already knew how to make deviled eggs, and it was a no-brainer to turn them into eyeballs and dub them Evil Eggs. And so on.

As I became a more experienced hostess, I branched out. I began by throwing the most obvious theme parties—holidays were my starting point. At first, Christmas was the only party I threw that truly qualified as over-the-top. I had my mother's example as inspiration, but where she was ever-elegant, I went in the other direction. Maybe we're all drawn to what we don't have—but I was into the kitschiest food and décor I could find. I decorated with plastic reindeer, tinsel, and fake snow. I served mini grilled cheese and mini peanut butter and jelly sandwiches, and I stacked up Krispy Kreme doughnuts to form a tree. There was always a punch bowl of store-bought eggnog, spiked of course.

At those Christmas parties we often had a white elephant gift exchange, where you bring the cheesiest present you can think of, like a Chia Pet, wrapped. Everyone draws a number. The person with number one is the first to choose a present. As everyone watches, he opens it. Then the person with number two can either open a new present, or take number one's present from him. And so on down the line. It always made for many laughs, especially the Christmas where we did a sex toy white elephant exchange.

For some reason I was a do-it-yourselfer from the start. It wasn't so much a reaction to the fully catered, fully staffed parties I grew up with so much as it was my way of being a homemaker. To watch me in the kitchen, you'd think that my mom had cooked the family dinner every night, which was not the case, although she's an excellent cook. No matter, I was determined to do it all.

I had to have people over. It all came about very logically. It's no fun to cook for yourself. And my friends were my family. When I used up all the obvious holidays, I needed more excuses to entertain, so I cast a wider net. I had premiere parties for every TV movie I was in—and in my twenties that was four times a year. (You know, the traditional *Watch Me Get Stabbed By a Jealous Classmate Party, Watch Me Try to Remember Who Killed My Boyfriend Party,* and *Watch Me Stab My Boyfriend Party.*)

But it still wasn't enough. So even though I hate football, one year I decided to host a Super Bowl party. About twenty people came over for chili and cornbread. (I had grown up eating chili at Chasen's, and so was fond of it and wanted to make my own. Coming to love chili at a place like Chasen's is a little like saying that the pool at the Four Seasons made you fall in love with swimming, but that was my reality.) It was such a success that I came to have a Super Bowl party every year. As the years went by, I branched out. I color-coordinated napkins and treats with whichever teams were playing. This was particularly challenging since I didn't know which side to root for, and if I represented both, certain guests were sure to object. Besides, football colors are pretty ghastly and including all four successfully was near impossible. When it came down to it, what choice did I really have? I simply picked the team with the prettier color combination.

Why was I having annual Super Bowl parties when I don't give a bean about football? Well, I had awakened the dormant homemaker gene hidden in the fiber of my soul. I was in love with throwing parties. Every aspect of it tapped into some inner compulsion. I loved the planning, the crafting, the cooking, getting deals, running out on the day of the party to make last-minute purchases, and the rush and thrill of getting everything in order just as the guests arrived. Throwing parties was genuinely fulfilling.

From the very beginning, my parties were about experimenting and having fun, not making checklists. What fun is a checklist? It limits you too much. That's what this book is about—the organic, inspiration-driven party.

Sure, a to-do list can help you remember everything that needs to get done, but we all know that. You don't need me to show you how to write a list of obvious tasks on a piece of paper. This book is meant to be inspirational, not simply instructional. Even so, I'll give you my tips and battlefield stories to show you how it's done (and what not to do—I have plenty of experience with that, too).

"GROWN-UP" PARTIES

Once I met my husband Dean, he became my guinea pig for refining my party-throwing technique. Before our kids were born, I threw one or two all-out birthday parties, and a couple other bonus gatherings. My favorite was Deano's Derby Day. About fifteen of us went to the racetrack. Wearing hats was mandatory. At the track, our table was decorated with little plastic trophies, and each seat had a mini racing form, which showed all our events for the day. After the fifth race, we all went to the Winner's Circle for a group photo.

Dean always liked his parties, but every year he said, "You don't have to go all out. Just keep it simple. I feel guilty when you work so hard." One year he was so emphatic in his protestations that I paused. It was Dean's birthday. Should I do what he wanted? But simple? I couldn't do simple. Simple was just him and me, sitting at dinner. Sure, I like that, but it doesn't say "Birthday!" with quite the enthusiasm that I feel. Did that mean I shouldn't throw a party at all? For advice I turned to my "gay husband" Mehran: "Dean doesn't want me to throw a big to-do, but I love doing it."

Mehran, ever wise, said, "Well, you're not doing the parties for him anyway, are you? You're doing them for yourself. Once he's there, he has a great time. So don't penalize yourself." Mehran was right. Dean didn't need to feel

guilty and I didn't need to feel unappreciated. I had my own selfish reasons for making his birthdays unforgettable and unique. And since the effort was in part for me, he could enjoy them without feeling like I'd gone overboard on his behalf.

After I had considerable practice throwing parties for Dean, Liam and Stella arrived. Having children meant many joyful things, not least of which was two more birthday parties to plan every year. My mission was laid out for me, and I chose to accept it.

tori's PICKS

FAVORITE FLOWER: peony

FAVORITE DRINK: Kir Royale

FAVORITE HORS D'OEUVRE: pigs in a blanket

FAVORITE FOOD: mac and cheese

FAVORITE COLOR COMBO: canary yellow and charcoal gray

BEST PARTY EVER: my thirtieth birthday party—it was an 80's prom party

FAVORITE GUEST: Jenny

FAVORITE HELPER: James

FAVORITE THEME: Marie Antoinette

FAVORITE DESSERT: any kind of fruit pie

BEST TIP THAT I ALWAYS DO: make everything a mini

BEST TIP THAT I NEVER MANAGE: leave time to get ready so you're dressed when the guests arrive

style and budget make friends

My parents threw some spectacular parties, including my first wedding. But opulence is not my thing. Over-the-top, yes. But I live in the real world (well, the "reality" world), where the coffers aren't exactly limitless. Besides, I like the feeling of working hard, being creative, and doing things myself. Spending huge amounts of money on a few hours of fun when you have three kids to put through school and life—it's just not practical. We can't live frivolously—we need to save. I like finding less expensive ways to achieve the effect I want.

Also, because I'm a working mom, I don't get to see my kids as much as I'd like. If I spent all my time out shopping for parties I'd never see them. In the rush of the holidays you can go out to pick up a couple items and find yourself trapped in a store with crowds of people for hours on end. Instead, I pick up materials, bring them home, and do projects with the kids. Last Christmas, instead of buying ornaments, I found empty glass ornaments made so that you could fill them with whatever you wanted. Stella, Liam, and I decorated them by inserting all sorts of feathers, fake snow, bits of tinsel, or loose glitter. I'd seen such glass ornaments at Crate & Barrel for more than twenty dollars. The ones we made probably cost a dollar each. And the time together? Priceless.

I love the puzzle of throwing special, chic parties with down-to-earth budgets, and, lucky you, I'm psyched to share my secrets.

PERSONAL TOUCHES

Anyone can have good taste. Nice, tasteful parties are a dime a dozen. And they're forgettable. How many times have you gone to a restaurant for a friend's birthday? Do any of those nights stand out in your memory? I didn't think so.

One of my closest girlfriends, Amy, recently got married. Eight of us co-hosted a bridal shower for her, but when it came to the planning, I let the other girls take the reins. As the date drew closer and I saw the party taking shape via email exchange, I said to my friend James, "What's wrong with me? I love Amy and this whole group. Why am I holding back?"

The answer is simple: I'm a control freak. I knew that in order to preserve my friendships, I couldn't take over the party and boss everyone around.

My friends have great taste, and the party was lovely. The invitations were chocolate brown and blue, very cool and chic. The shower was a luncheon at Cecconi's, the classic Italian restaurant in West Hollywood. There was a champagne toast, appetizers, lunch, and a piece of gourmet chocolate bark as a favor in front of each person. It was a luncheon. It was nice. There just wasn't anything that screamed Amy, and I missed that. I'm all about the personal touches. Amy loves traveling. In particular she likes Spain and Spanish food, especially Manchego cheese and jamón serrano. If I'd done her party I might have made invitations out of fans. I probably would have had a cheese tasting bar and served all the food tapas-style. There would have been chocolate-dipped churros for dessert, and maybe I would have put castanets at every place setting with a little tag saying, "Please click when the guest of honor enters the room." Maybe I would have put a Spanish cookie in the mouth of each castanet . . . I could go on. Which is probably why it was better for me to hold back.

But I was horrified to hear that those favors were ten dollars each. For a few bites of chocolate! With no handmade tags! That was crazy to me.

For me, it all comes down to creativity. Along with Dean and my friend James, I have been planning weddings for a show called *Tori & Dean: sTORIbook Weddings.* The third wedding that we put together was an Argentinian wedding. James had ordered a black chunky picture frame for each table in order to display the table number. We had already used frames in this manner for the first two weddings. I was at my limit with the frames. Then, when I saw them set out, I wasn't happy. They looked too modern. The wedding had a clean, elegant look, with white roses and delicate lines. Those frames were just . . . wrong. I wanted to come up with something different—an entirely new concept for displaying the table numbers. James, on the other hand, comes from a set-design background. If something looks good and works, he wants to move ahead with it. He thought the frames were fine and wanted to check them off his list. When he tried to convince me, we kind of fought. Finally I said, "Are the frames great or do they work?"

James paused. He said, "They work." And from then on he understood what I was going for. (For that wedding we ended up using simple, thin, wrought-iron frames. They were *much* better.)

That's my motto now: *Is it great or does it work?* When guests walk into one of my parties, I want them to be transported into a whole new world. The details matter, even small things like frames, elements you would think nobody notices. If it just works, I go back to the drawing board. You don't have to be as into it as I am, but I encourage you to strive for *great,* and fall back on *it works.*

I look around and think that the world we live in is too generic. We all look the same, dress the same, eat the same foods, and throw the same parties. I'm tired of jeans and beer. I look at vintage pictures of parties and

marvel at the caftans and martinis. True, maybe that was equally generic for them. Maybe caftans and martinis were the jeans and beer of their day. And maybe it felt good for that generation to let go of the formality and kick back in the freedom of a dressed-down life, but I think something was lost in translation. I look back at what was beautiful, well-made, and unique, find inspiration, and reinvent what I see to make it current and chic.

It's all about creativity, about slowing down and taking the time to come up with ideas. It's hard to sit down and let yourself brainstorm. I like to go to the store, see what they have, flit around the Web, keep moving forward. But true creativity stretches your imagination. Try it, it feels great.

They say the devil's in the details, but for me the details are heaven. Maybe an avid planner and host like me should say that in the course of the party I'm on a cloud of joy, but that would be a lie. Planning and preparing are my favorite parts of the process. Truth be told, when it comes to the actual parties, I'm a nervous wreck. But there is a moment of joy. Mine comes when I see the party come together. The guests are flowing through the space, tasting food, trying out any activities, having conversations with friends and strangers. And when I see someone take a bite of dessert, or try out a photo booth costume, or smile as they pick up a favor, well, that makes it all worth it.

Creating a party. It's my favorite thing to do, and I'm inviting you, as my guest, to join me in the festivities. I know we're going to have fun. Come—discover your inner party planner!

Love

Jni

part one:
ESSENTIALS

The first step in planning any party is working out the five questions:

Who

What

When

Where

Why

You have to figure out these core elements before you get to the fun stuff.

what's your excuse?

Something has inspired you to plan a get-together. Is it a birthday, an anniversary, a milestone, a holiday, or is it just the primal desire to gather your tribe? Your reason is your launch pad. It sets the guest list and sends you on your way toward answering the other four questions.

the guest list

Once you have a purpose, it's time to decide who is in and who is—as Heidi Klum would say—out. The size of your party can really affect the cost. Etiquette experts keep it simple by saying that you should make the guest list first, then see what you can afford. But we all know it's never that simple. The list of potential invitees can sprawl on forever. At some point you have to draw a line between A list and B list.

There's nothing I fear more than offending someone, so I err on the side of over-inviting. I invite everyone who might hear about the party and care if they weren't invited. When I first joined a moms' book club, I only really knew three people in it. But I invited all twelve of the moms to my next party. My friend Carrie said, "You invited everyone? You're nicer than I am." When the book club moms showed up, I didn't even recognize some of them. We had to reintroduce ourselves. They seemed to be wondering why they were there. It was weird and awkward. I learned a vital lesson, which I now pass on to you: Only invite people you recognize (and their significant others).

lay claim TO A DAY

If you don't have a genuine excuse for a party, all the better. Invent a reason and make it your own. Why do you think I used to have an annual Super Bowl party? I'm certainly not a football fan. But dreary February is an excellent month for a party, and I had already done Valentine's Day. Find a list of obscure holidays and celebrate the one that's approaching, be it the Australian Queen's birthday, National Puzzle Day, or Mayflower Day. There's even a Space Day. I can already see the gift bags with punched-out stars and dehydrated astronaut ice cream as favors. If your party's a hit, bring it back every year. Make it famous, or infamous. Take pictures and show them to your grandkids: "Here, Sonny, is me at the tenth annual Pigs Can Fly party. Someday you'll pick up the torch."

My friend Jeff Lewis gave me an invaluable tip about making a guest list. Make sure everyone on your list will know at least one other person at the party. This guarantees that they will have someone to turn to for conversation other than you. Even as they boldly venture out to talk to new people, they will have a home base. A singleton becomes your responsibility. You'll spend all night worrying about him.

Don't be petty about guest lists—they can make or break friendships. My six best male friends are Mehran, the "Guncles" (Bill and Scout, who are gay "uncles" to my kids), Marcel, James, and Gueran. I always want them all to be close friends with one another, but while there is some cross-pollination, they aren't all equally friends. James and the Guncles have a little rivalry. It's all jokey and friendly, but it puts me in the middle. When James and I were trying to remember how the friction started, he said, "Oh, I know! They didn't invite me to Mehran's birthday dinner this year."

I said, "But that dinner has been the same group every year for years!"

Then James said, "No, I remember what it was. Two years ago *I* didn't invite *them* to my birthday dinner at Café Stella. They found out about it and I think they were hurt. But I have the same people every year."

Could it be? That all the semiserious conflict stemmed from one party invitation or another? See what happens when I mix my gays? The point is that you have to be careful. As a host, think about the feelings of your wider social circle. And as a slighted guest, let it go. Be inclusive and forgive. Do as I say, not as I do.

So make your guest list, and decide if your party is going to be:

- A small party (less than 15)

- A medium party (15–30)

- A bash (more than 30)

KIDS OR *no kids*

At this point in my life, with three little kids, one of the first decisions I make about any celebration is whether it's going to be a kid-friendly hullabaloo or a strictly adult affair. This book focuses on adult parties, but to me that doesn't exclude kids. It just means it isn't a party created primarily for kids. As my kids age, I hope that they and their friends will be with us at more and more social events.

The very first and critical element of a kid-friendly gathering is timing. If you're having a mixed-ages evening event, just make sure it starts early. The earlier the better. Start it at five, serve mac and cheese, and your friends (except the inevitable ones whose kids have dairy allergies) will love you forever.

Obviously, kids affect every aspect of a party. You're not going to lounge and drink martinis with kids around. You're going to lounge and *carefully place your martini* on a bar-height table, out of reach of little hands. If kids are in attendance, their parents' ability to enjoy a party depends, well, on their ages and personalities. Sometimes nothing can be done. Providing a glass of wine always helps. Arranging several long, engaging activities for kids is another solution. Ideally, there will be some indestructible area of the house or yard to which the children can be relegated to entertain themselves for stretches of time while you cram in the eating, drinking, and conversation that you took for granted before those darling angels entered your life.

the perfect prescription

We're going to take your party notion and ratchet it up to a full-on *concept,* but you need to pick a direction in order to move forward. Ask yourself the following questions to figure out what you want: Is it big or small? Quiet or loud? Casual or fancy? When people walk into the party, do I want them to feel warm and comfortable or chic and fabulous? Do I want to spend the night introducing people and making matches, or do I want to gather people who know one another and can take care of themselves? Do I imagine my guests lounging with colorful martinis or doing the limbo on a leopard-patterned dance floor?

Choose your function (brunch, lunch, tea, etc.) based on the vibe and formality you want. A weekend brunch is the first stop on a day of leisure. It often has a laid-back, hungover feel, whether guests are hungover or not. Conversation is relaxed. People think of it as a midpoint in their day.

Cocktails can and should be served any time, day or night, but the cocktail hour (traditionally six to eight) is one where people are lively and adventurous. The night is young. Anything might happen. In terms of vibe, a cocktail party is the opposite of brunch.

At a dinner party, even if it's a buffet, your guests are in for the long haul. They've committed their evening to you, often a weekend evening, and you owe it to them to give them a solid return on that investment. A dinner party has a timetable with multiple phases: cocktails, the meal, dessert, and after-dinner drinks. The best dinner parties sparkle with new interactions and funny, stimulating conversations. But they can also go wrong, making your guests feel trapped in an airplane that's endlessly delayed. Ah, the dinner party. It holds the greatest risk, and the greatest potential reward.

Choose one category from each column, and you'll have a description of your event. For example: An intimate shower to be held in the afternoon, or blowout birthday cocktails.

size	event	function
Intimate (less than 15 guests)	Birthday	Brunch
Medium (15–30 guests)	Holiday	Lunch
Blowout (more than 30 guests)	Shower	Afternoon
	Achievement	Cocktails
	Other	Dinner
		Other

set the date and time

Don't be cavalier when you schedule the party. Take a moment to figure out what will work best for you. What time of year is it? What will the temperature be? Do you want it to take place inside or outside? If it will be outside, do you want your party to take place before the sun goes down? Also consider your schedule. Look at the week leading up to your party. Is it relatively uncluttered? Will you have time the day before to shop, cook, prep, and set up? Now is the time to call a few key guests to make sure they'll be free, especially the ones who are your go-to helpers!

We've already talked generally about what time of day the party will occur. Now pinpoint the hour, and whether you will give an end-time on the invitation.

MY FAVORITE START TIMES

Brunch: I like brunch from 11–1.

Afternoon party: In summer, start at 4 P.M., when the sun isn't quite as hot. In winter, you start at 3 P.M. to maximize daylight hours.

Cocktail party: I start cocktails at 7 P.M., but if many guests are bringing children, I'll start an hour earlier at 6.

Dinner party: I always do cocktails at 7 P.M. and dinner an hour later, at 8. Again, I move everything an hour earlier if children are attending.

Dessert and champagne party: What? A party without salt and carb overload? I'm totally against it. I would be miserable. I'll take a cocktail weenie over a cupcake any day.

Now you've decided the who, what, why, and when of your party. Next you must decide where it will all go down.

the most special place of all

The setting of your party is crucial. You want it to be luxe, but affordable. You want it to be gorgeous, but comfortable. You want total control, but you don't want to work too hard. You want it to be special, but personal. You want it to be convenient, a place where you can come and go as you please, set up early, and stay until you drink the dregs. What would you say if I told you that all this can be yours in your very own home? Wait, wait, wait. You must consider this. People are so afraid of their own homes! But unless you're having a blowout bash and there simply isn't room for the bodies, chances are you can make your space work—not just make it work: Make it great!

If you rent a venue or host at a restaurant, your options are limited. First of all, it costs a fortune, which means you can't spend money on personal touches. And with a venue, there are limited details you can control. You have to use their food, their bar, and their furnishings. Even if they let you bring in some décor, setup can't be done in advance. You'll have to cart anything you prepare there and back. You won't bother with customizing details like candles, linens, glassware, or specialty foods and beverages. You'll just sign on to their cookie-cutter party and hope for the best. That's all fine and good, but it's not very ambitious. Am I right?

Having a party at home is extremely cost-effective. You can pick up food at an inexpensive store like Costco or Trader Joe's. If you don't have serving dishes you can borrow them from friends. You can even make it potluck. (I can't ever host potluck because I can't relinquish control, but I know that normal people without control issues enjoy them immensely.)

I'm glad we got that resolved. Party's at your place. Think of all that money you're saving. Now let's spend it.

{saving money}
AT OUTSIDE VENUES

If you really must have your party outside your home, here are a few hints to cut costs.

- **SPACE.** Look for a restaurant with a patio or a side room. It's generally easier to rent a partial space than a whole restaurant.

- **DAY.** Most of the time you can get a space for less money if you schedule your event on a Sunday. Fridays and Saturdays are when restaurants do their biggest business. You're more likely to get a good rate on a slower day.

- **TIME.** The same rule of thumb goes for time of day. If you ask a hotel to do an event from 4–6 P.M., after lunch has finished and before the dinner crowd has arrived, they realize it's a dead time for them. If a restaurant doesn't ordinarily serve breakfast, ask to do an event from 10–12 P.M. Your brunch will bring in extra money, even if they give you a deal.

So to manage your budget, work with your venue and be flexible with time. If it's cheaper, it's worth it.

a new word for me: budget

Nobody decides to have a party with a fixed budget in mind—unless you're doing it for a TV show (which I'll admit is not alien to me) or having a wedding and there's a benefactor involved. (Thanks, Mom, it *was* a beautiful wedding—even if it happened to be the wrong, but very nice, guy.) Let's be practical—we all have different ideas of what a dollar is worth and, maybe more critically, how it should be spent. I can't tell you how much to spend on your party. My biggest tip across the board for saving money is to start from scratch. The more you do things yourself, the slower the costs will add up and the more fun you can have. This is true when it comes to your food, your décor, and your serving pieces.

FOOD AND SHOPPING

The best way to save money on food is to make fewer dishes. Pull a number of recipes that interest you, then edit yourself. Be realistic. Think about how long the party will last and how much an average person eats. Sure, it's good to have an overabundance of food, but not a wasteful amount. And you certainly don't want to buy ingredients for a recipe that you end up having no time left to make. Go to the store with a set menu and a shopping list.

This may sound obvious, but before you go to the store, check to see which ingredients you already have at home. I must have six jars of cinnamon because I never remember to check before I'm at the store shopping for ingredients for eggnog. Little extras like that, especially spices, clutter your kitchen and add up on the grocery bill.

Prepared or premade food cuts down on time, but it costs you more. You'll pay a premium for those hideous plastic platters with cut-up carrots, celery, and ranch dip in the middle. Save money by peeling the carrots and cutting them up yourself. Cheaper, and fresher. If you must get the premade platter, that's okay. But please, I beg you, transfer its contents to your own dish. Anything is better than that store-bought clear plastic.

BEVERAGES

Even for a daytime party, I always buy soda in liter bottles instead of six-packs. I found that when I offered cans, guests would take a few sips, put down the can, and forget about it. When people have the freedom to pour their own drinks, they can take exactly the amount they want. There is only one critical exception to this rule: You should absolutely buy individual sodas if you are color-coordinating the bottles.

I can't stand the look of those ubiquitous water bottles, and you know they must be dominating landfills across the country. Instead of buying individual water bottles, fill pitchers with your favorite water. Or invest in one of those glass water coolers with a button you push to serve yourself. It looks much better and saves plastic.

In my twenties, I thought I had to offer every kind of liquor known to man at my parties. The built-in bar in my apartment must have been five feet long, and lined up on it were what I thought were the standard liquors. Some were—vodka, gin, tequila, scotch. And some not so much—Jägermeister, Goldschläger, Bailey's. I bought mega bottles of them at Costco and supplemented with wine coolers. Wine coolers! Not exactly the beverage choice of a sophisticated host.

At my parties now I don't put any bottles of liquor out for my guests. Instead, I offer one or two premade cocktails and wine. If I do put liquor out, I decant vodka and gin into nice bottles with labels. If I serve beer it's mostly Stella Artois—because of my daughter Stella and because I think foreign beer looks more chic.

DISHES AND GLASSWARE

Don't wait until you're having a party to stock your kitchen with dishes and glassware. If you love garage sales as much as I do (and you should, they are a host's dream come true!), you can start building a collection of mismatched finds that will look great at any party.

I'm going to go out on a limb here. In a world of overshopping and clutter, I say that buying more (at least at garage sales) can save you money in the long run. You just have to develop a discerning eye.

You don't need to buy or own full sets of anything. If you're at a garage sale, and you see two glasses you love for a dollar, buy them. A mishmash collection is cool and chic.

Scavenge glassware and plates that suit your own taste. If your interests are wide, rein them in. You can't mix an uber-modern square plate with a floral Wedgwood plate. You can mix decades within reason, but it's easiest to stay within a style or era. If you like florals, it's absolutely great to mismatch them. I happen to love Georges Briard glassware, which has gold deco details, and hobnail milk glass, which is bumpy and opaque. If I ever spot any of these items at a flea market or garage sale, I snap it up.

It's very hard for me to drive past a garage sale. The anticipation of discovering lost treasures is irresistible. One time I was driving home over Laurel Canyon, late as usual, and I saw a garage sale. I slowed down to see if

it looked promising. But from my window it looked like a hot mess, so I kept going up the street. A block later I found myself pulling a U-turn. So what if it was a hot mess? I had to make sure I wasn't missing anything.

I was right—the Laurel Canyon garage sale was all junk. Then, huddled in the forgotten corner of a dusty bookshelf, I found a little hobnail milk glass candy dish in perfect condition. It had to be worth thirty or forty dollars. But here it was three dollars! My own *Antiques Roadshow* moment. I tried not to show my excitement for fear they'd raise the price. As I drove away with my newfound treasure, I smiled in satisfaction. I had learned my lesson that day. Never judge a yard sale prematurely. There's always a find waiting to be rescued. From then on I knew to stop every single time.

Okay, so it's probably not wise to be as reckless and obsessed as I am. There's a reason I have a storage space that I have to empty out and sell from every few years. Instead, I suggest you scout for a while, see where your passion lies, pick out a few finds, and bring them home to see if they all look nice together. The trick is to keep in mind the storage space you have and the type of parties you like to throw. My hobnail milk glass doesn't work with my Georges Briard glass. The milk glass is white and whimsical. It's more feminine. The deco glass is for nighttime cocktails. If you're just getting started you should pick one direction or another. If you stick to your favorites, you will slowly build an amazing and unique collection that will give your parties character and style.

These budget-saving tips get to the heart of what I'm trying to tell you about parties and life in general. The point is to break away from the plain, generic direction we all seem to be following. Trust your instincts. Develop your taste. Be unique. Bring color and disorder and spirit into your life, and it will seep into your parties.

part two:

GETTING
STARTED

This is my favorite part. It's time to choose a theme. Except that I hate the word *theme*. When I was planning my first wedding, I was describing my vision to my mother. I wanted a twenties, *Great Gatsby* feel to the night. My mother said, "Well, this isn't Disneyland. We're not having a *theme* party." She made *theme* sound like a bad word. So let's keep it a little more sophisticated. I'm really talking about a driving vision or inspiration. I'm going to call it a *concept*. In this section I'll help you pick a concept and we'll choose the key elements to bring that concept to life.

your mood board

It's possible that I like planning a party more than I enjoy the party itself. To be honest, I'm the same way about decorating. Every time I go on vacation, I see a house or store or bed-and-breakfast, etc. that I want to buy and decorate. It's unclear if I would truly enjoy having a ski lodge in the mountains, but boy do I want to pick out the mantelpiece and sheepskin rugs.

When I plan a party, I start by making a *mood board.* Does that sound overwhelming? Let me break it down for you.

The biggest mistake people make when planning parties is to act before they think. Don't rush to make any decisions about how your party will look and feel or what will happen there. I like to take some time to sit with the idea. I carry it around with me, like a little wrapped box from jeweler Neil Lane that I'm just waiting to open. (Hint, hint, Dean!)

When you have time, flip through magazines or look on the Web for images that inspire you. They don't have to be specifically party-related images, like flower arrangements or a cluster of candles. They can be more open-ended, like a painting that sets the mood you'd like to have, or a shot from a movie with a distinct style, or a combination of colors that catches your eye. Pull all your images into a folder—real or virtual.

At this stage—the brainstorming phase—your ideas don't have to connect at all. The collection of ideas that you compile doesn't have to serve this party alone. Sure, every image you find might end up setting the tone for your Bon Voyage party, but they also might languish for years in the folder until you have that Resort Chic party of your dreams.

When I'm brainstorming, I pull all kinds of images that resonate with me in terms of the look and feel of the party. Maybe it's a scene from a silent movie. Maybe it's a photo of a tropical island. Maybe it's an image of a garden or something as specific as a centerpiece. Style. Color. Graphics.

Once you have a nice, thick folder, take an evening to let a concept evolve. Spread all your clippings out over a table. Do you notice any unifying elements? Are you drawn to sorbet colors? Do you go for a stark, minimalist look? Are all your pictures of cake? Now pare your findings down to a few images—maybe ten or so—that will steer this party. Paste them all to a poster board. This is your mood board and it defines your concept. You must name this concept, even if you don't know whether it's Neoclassical, Art Deco, or Grunge (say it isn't so). Call it Swirly-Whirl, for all I care. (But please don't tell your guests that based on Tori Spelling's advice you're having a Swirly-Whirl party.)

{trainwreck}

SNAY DAY

A Winter Wonderland party. When I was five years old, my father famously had a hill of snow made in our backyard for a white Christmas in sunny, warm Los Angeles. At the time, if snowmakers even existed, they were massive industrial machines exclusively seen at ski resorts. The white Christmas that my father made for me was an unforgettable moment in my childhood. And now that importing snow was less of a challenge, I decided I wanted to do the same for my kids—to have a snow day in our backyard for Liam, Stella, and a bunch of children from the Ronald McDonald House. There would be icebergs floating in the pool, reindeer strolling the lawn, and, of course, the requisite hill for sledding fun. We would serve McDonald's food, but on silver platters (my mom would have been proud).

As much as it doesn't snow, it doesn't rain often in Los Angeles, but our snow day happened to fall after two days of heavy rain. The lawn was absolutely saturated. Then they put beautiful man-made snow on top of it. But as we set up the backyard, the food vendors rolled their carts across the snow, sinking through to the grass and mud beneath. Soon enough all the snow on the grass around the pool was gone, and in its place: slush. Four inches of icy brown slush.

Now the night before the party I was out very late, filming a cameo on the new *90210* with my friend Jennie Garth until three in the morning. But I didn't worry. I had lined up James and the Guncles to meet the people delivering the snow. And the food was donated—it was a charity event—so I didn't have to worry about that either.

I slept in, and by the time I woke up the backyard had a huge snowy hill in it. I'd never seen snow in our backyard, of course, and I never would again. It was beautiful. But encircling the pool, where I expected to see snow, was . . . *hay*. My friends James and Marcel had been desperate to find a way to absorb the slush. They had taken some extra hay bales left over from the ones the snowmaking company had used to build the sledding hill, and spread it out over the lawn.

I cried.

Our winter wonderland was a boggy hayfield. Hence *Snay Day.*

The guests arrived and everyone oohed and aahed at the sledding hill, but I was devastated. Some winter wonderland. There was hay and slush all over the backyard! My best friend Jenny tried to comfort me, saying, "Look at the kids. They're having a great time. Do they look upset? It doesn't matter." But from then on I had a standard by which to measure every party disaster. Would it be better than Snay Day?

{tori TIP... NEVER WEAR HEELS TO AN OUTDOOR PARTY. STICK TO WEDGES.

The iPad has a mood board app that allows you to drag and drop images onto a digital board. Yes, an iPad is expensive, but if it isn't out of reach it allows you to have the entire Web as your digital photo library. Using magazines and poster board works just as well. But if you have access to an iPad, try it. You'll love it.

The first mood board I made was when I was planning a wedding for the Guncles. I asked them to pick a color they liked, and they gave me a peacock blue swatch. I put that on the empty board and let it be my inspiration. The wedding was going to be outside in Palm Springs, so I looked for images that fit with that setting. If an image looked wrong when displayed with the rest of it, I ripped it off. As I picked and chose, I started to get a feel for what the wedding would be and began to paste my favorites on the board. There was a picture of parasols clustered in a box. A photo of lanterns hinted at dark, clustered lighting as opposed to something bright like chandeliers. I found a shot of a wish tree, where each guest could write a wish on a paper leaf and hang it for the grooms. There were photos of outdoor seating, a box-shaped cake, and a table runner with a monogram at one end. Scout loves cheese so I pulled an image of a dessert table that I thought could be redone with cheese. There was a shot of a gray suit that I thought would look good with the peacock blue, hints of yellow, and dark wood. By the time I was done I felt like I had my work cut out for me. The Guncles ended up with tan suits, but for the most part that board was my guide. It told the whole story of what the wedding would be.

Liam and Stella are already in training to make their own mood boards one day. When I asked Liam what he likes in a party, he said, "Eating cheese. And I like red, and blue, and blue-black."

Stella chimed in, "I like presents."

color me festive

The simplest and least expensive way to develop your concept is to use color. A unifying color palette immediately sets a mood. When you walk into a space and see coordinated pops of color, you know that you are in the hands of an organized, tasteful host who cares about your experience, has thought it through, and is about to show you a good time. (Not *that* kind of good time. Please.)

{color} COMBINATION

HERE ARE SOME OF MY FAVORITE COLOR COMBINATIONS:

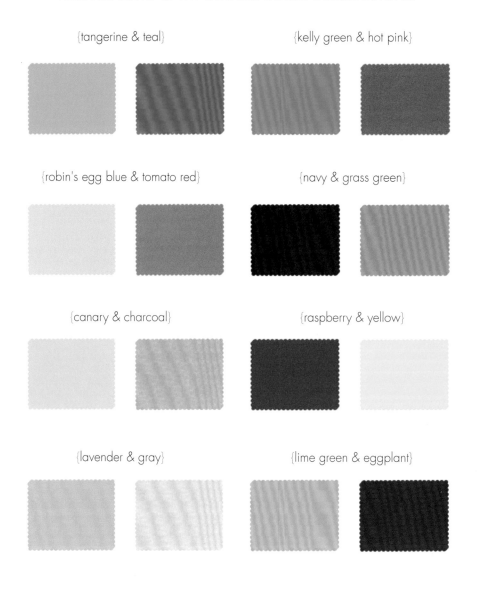

{tangerine & teal}

{kelly green & hot pink}

{robin's egg blue & tomato red}

{navy & grass green}

{canary & charcoal}

{raspberry & yellow}

{lavender & gray}

{lime green & eggplant}

Your color choice can make or break your party. Pink and brown used to be chic, but now I think it's overdone. Purple and red is horrendous. Recently I threw a party and had what I thought was the innovative idea of using fuchsia and lime green. It looked amazing, but after the party I noticed that color combination everywhere. It was still a great party, but I was disappointed that I hadn't been the one to launch the trend.

The color scheme is driven by the guest of honor or the purpose of the party. If your party is celebrating a person's birthday or a couple's anniversary, you need to think about what that person likes. If I were having a party for Jenny, I'd pick classic colors that are in her comfort zone. For Mehran I'd play with fuchsia and gold—maybe an Arabian Nights scheme. When Liam wanted a superhero party, I picked red and blue, which felt like iconic superhero colors.

There is a tipping point for color. If you use it to highlight the key points of your party, it pulls the space together and gives the party a feeling of deliberateness. Your guests realize that you have a plan. They put themselves and their time into your hands.

Try to implement your colors in the following aspects of your party:

- Invitations
- Tables
- Flowers

- Pillows, fabrics
- Napkins, glassware

- Cocktails
- Dessert table
- Signage

YOU'RE INVITED

Think how far you've come. You know the answers to the basic questions: who, what, when, where, and why. You've picked a concept—and I bet you never even knew your party needed one! And you've selected your colors. See what I mean about stretching your imagination? That's a lot of planning without actually buying or making anything. Now we get to the fun part.

LIMIT THE *cheesiness factor*

I like a party with a concept. Okay, I'm absolutely mad for concept-driven parties. But even I know that there's such a thing as going overboard. I want you to go over-the-top, but I still want you to keep it classy. Here are some guidelines:

do	*don't*
do maximize your color scheme.	*don't* buy out the Internet with any and everything related to your concept. Get the lay of the land before you make any purchases.
do dress according to your concept.	*don't* take on some concept-related personality, like speaking with a Spanish accent at a fiesta party.
do applaud guests for participating in the concept.	*don't* require guests to participate in the concept, or express disappointment if they choose not to do so.
do go all out with concept-related desserts.	*don't* spend so much time on your concept that you forget the basics.
do aim for total immersion, driven by your color scheme.	*don't* lose track of elegance and style. Don't buy the St. Paddy's candles if they have a hideous plastic leprechaun. Plain candles are fine . . . unless you track down elegant shamrock votives.

down with EVITE

When I get an electronic invitation or an invitation through Facebook, I don't even open it. It's vulgar! Down with Evite, I say. I get it. It's easy. It's fast. It allows you to manage RSVPs. There are many benefits to using Evite, Facebook, or any other online service to send invitations. But if I teach you anything, it should be that *easiest* isn't *best*. I mean, come on. The invitation is the first thing a guest sees. It sets the mood for the party. It sets the *concept* for the party. If you are reading this book, it means you aren't lazy. You *care*. You're going to all the trouble to make a party that feels special, so the very least you can do is send a proper invitation.

If you've ever sent an Evite, haven't you noticed that of all the hundreds of invitations you can choose from, the one you want just doesn't exist? That's because you are a unique, special person. Your party is a unique, special event. It deserves more. This isn't a wedding. You don't have to go all out and have a custom invitation printed up. In the real world there are plenty of nice, inexpensive invitations you can buy. Even if they aren't one hundred percent original, they look nicer. They arrive by mail with a handwritten envelope. They feel real and special. Your guests can respond by phone or email. They are grown-ups. They can do it. And you can handle the responses, easy as pie. If you must invite by email, just send an email. Attach a photo that is meaningful to you.

Let's tell the world—actually, just that very special part of the world whom you've decided to include—that this event is actually going down.

WHAT TO INCLUDE

It should be obvious, but I have to say it: Make sure your invitation includes all the critical information—who, what, when, and where. Don't forget RSVP information, and include directions if finding the location is at all challenging. Please proofread. A typo on an invitation is just horrifying.

Including how you'd like people to dress for the party creates anticipation. For an outdoor party, I've asked people to wear garden attire. The Guncles' wedding was resort chic. Even if you're just telling your guests to wear cocktail attire, try to find a more creative way to express it. For an Oscar party you could suggest that they wear "Oscar gold" or dress glam. For a different outdoor party, I asked people to wear summer florals.

SETTING THE TONE

The invitation to your party is the first impression, and you know what they say about first impressions. (Wait, what *do* they say about first impressions? Don't judge a book by its cover? Whatever. You know what I mean.) Your invitation sets the tone for your event, and now that you have one, your invitation should introduce your concept—especially color.

First, let's talk about the form of delivery. Evites and other electronic invitations have become enormously popular. We all know why. They are super-convenient. While an electronic invitation might be practical for a huge, informal event, like a school auction, there is nothing special about it. Let me repeat that. Nothing special, right out the door. Who wants that?

If you're having a small party, do not fear the phone. The phone is not only a perfectly acceptable means of communication, but it actually makes your guests know how special they are, to be included at this very select event. It also allows you to get an early gauge on attendance. Keep a list of responses. And, yes, it's fine to confirm by email to say "Looking forward to seeing you at Dean's Moto-Madness Party!" about a week before the event.

Handwritten notes to your guests are an even more sophisticated way of inviting them to an event and can be a particularly nice touch of old-world elegance.

Do not rule out the possibility of store-bought invitations. There are so many lovely ones out there to choose from. They should be simple and clean, but chic. The ones that are letterpress (with sunken letters and images) or embossed (with raised letters and images) are nicer than flat invites. Look for thick, heavy paper. Unlike online invitations, you can personalize an otherwise simple invitation by finding postal stamps that fit with your concept and using them to prettify the envelope.

Even more unusual and impressive than a well-chosen stamp is a wax seal. I mean, we should all use a wax seal at least once in our lifetimes, right? One party. One wax seal. Please?

Invitations are small and self-contained—a perfect place to stretch your imagination. There are infinite ways you can make them personal. You can create them by hand. You can incorporate small objects that are teasers for the big event. You can search for premade invitations that perfectly capture the party you envision. Start out strong. Take the time to get it right. Enjoy the process. You are taking the first step in creating a one-of-a-kind event. Deliver that promise right into the homes of the invitees. And soon enough they will be delivering themselves into your home . . . and now we're going to make sure you've created an amazing world to greet them when they arrive.

{over-the-top} INVITATIONS

An invitation is not just informational. It is a seduction and a promise. This party *will* be amazing, and you *will* have a good time. A small party is an opportunity to do an over-the-top invitation by including a little taste of what's to come, sometimes literally. For a fiesta party, include a packet of margarita salt. For a New Year's Eve party, include shiny confetti and ribbons. For a beach party, dab glue on the invite and sprinkle with sand. Include an aspirin for a hangover party. Think about the senses: What taste, smell, sound, feel, or sight will transport your would-be guests to the party you are just beginning to envision? Or give them something to play with. Any hint of the party to come is tantalizing. What an easy way to have fun.

STELLA'S SEEDS

~Alyssum Flowers~

Seed Depth: Press into surface
Light: Direct sunlight
Watering: Daily with love
Temperature: 70-80 Degre

our little ladybug
is turning 1!

*Come celebrate
Stella's Birthday*

please join us for
a stroll in the garden
and a ladybug luncheon

11-2pm
saturday, june 6th
2 0 0 9

. . .

part three:
DÉCOR

The moment you enter the room, you feel transported. There is a sense of excitement and cohesion. Around the room are different vignettes, all of which are tied together. A color scheme sets the tone. Candles flicker with that ever-flattering indirect light. Handmade signs gently guide you through the space. Empty glassware is set out in neat lines, soon to be filled one by one. Yummy smells emanate from the kitchen. A decadent dessert table tells you to indulge to your heart's delight. And a cluster of fabulous favor bags reminds you throughout the party that you will take a little bit of it home with you. Sigh.

Designing the event—as an experience that is both planned and full of spontaneity—is my favorite part.

setting the party zone

The first step in arranging your party is preparing the space. If you follow my instructions below, you may end up rearranging your space considerably, and you'll want to have a chance to clean behind and beneath everything that gets moved. I recommend envisioning your plan well in advance, then moving furniture and cleaning the space up to an entire week before the date of the party. Trust me, if you spend the whole day of your party making big changes, by the time your guests arrive you'll be too exhausted to enjoy yourself. I know, because that's what I stupidly do every time.

STATIONS AND FLOW

Consider the room or rooms where you expect guests to congregate. Now imagine the party area completely empty. We're starting from scratch.

Think about the points of activity at your party. When people first come in, they may need to put down their coats. Create a space near the door where you will direct them to do so—preferably in a side room that isn't being used for the party. If you don't have space, be creative. It's fine to hang coats on a strong shower curtain bar. If you live in an apartment, buy or borrow a cheap coat rack that you can put outside the door.

Next your guests will want drinks. Where will they get them? The bar should be the first station that guests see when they're getting oriented. It should be far enough from the door to draw people into the party space, and it should be in as open a space as possible so that the people who inevitably get stuck talking right there, drink in hand, don't create a logjam.

Your main food station should be as far from the bar as possible. This draws people through and across the space. On their way from one to the other, they may encounter friends or escape from boring conversations.

Now imagine your party as a triangle. The bar and the main food table form the two base points, and the dessert table, always my crowning glory, is the top. Dessert comes last, so it should feel a little farther into the party, in a special place that guests will be drawn to visit.

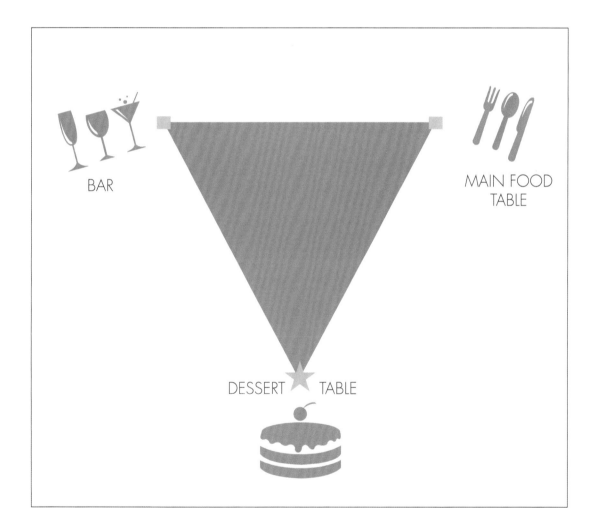

BAR

MAIN FOOD
TABLE

DESSERT ★ TABLE

Additionally, you will want to have a couple other places to put nibbles of food, a few separate areas for lounging (space permitting), and you may have an activity station—I have some suggestions ahead.

Ideally, you pick where the three main events happen (drinks, food, dessert), add in the additional elements (lounging, activity stations), and move your existing furniture to accommodate them.

MOVE MOUNTAINS

Unless your furniture is built-in (which I doubt, but if it is, aren't you fabulous?), you have infinite possibilities to change the way the space works. If you are not having a sit-down dinner, start by moving all your dining chairs out of the party space. This lets people circulate around the table or gives you the option to push the table against a wall. You'll still use the table as a food station, but this creates more space in the middle of the room.

Assess if there is any other furniture you should move out of the space. If you expect people to stand for most of the party, remove low cocktail tables. If you are worried about overcrowding, remove standing lamps.

DECLUTTER

Once you have an idea of the furniture and tabletops you want to accommodate your party, you should try to strip the excess. If you're expecting a rowdy crowd, remove anything precious and breakable. Aim to clear off all surfaces completely. To create an even cleaner look, remove lamps that you don't plan to turn on and decorative pieces that don't work with your concept.

CLEAN

All this moving of furniture and clutter will stir up the dust a bit, which is a good thing. If you get an early enough start, a party is a great excuse to do a deep cleaning. Vacuum. Dust bookshelves. Clean windows inside and out. Sure, any flaws will be hidden in the soft, forgiving lighting you'll soon plan, but isn't it nice to know that the windows will sparkle and a guest won't encounter dust bunnies if he stoops to retrieve a dropped cocktail napkin?

Remember that almost all of your guests will use the bathroom at least once. This is an unusual increase in activity for your poor bathroom and it's bound to suffer a bit. It should be spotless to begin with. Put two extra rolls of toilet paper out, just in case. And make sure everything is in good working order. Supply nice paper or cloth napkins for hand-drying, and a receptacle for used ones. If you opt for paper napkins, you can find a rubber stamp that goes well with your concept—a starfish for a beach party or a letter as a monogram—and stamp each napkin. It's another personal detail that looks nice.

MAKING OUTSIDE WORK

Outdoor parties can be spectacular, but most people with backyards don't have enough furniture for parties. Don't hesitate to bring the inside outside. Nothing is more chic. Move real furniture into your backyard, especially lounge-y sofas and armchairs, but even formal, traditional chairs are pleasingly ironic in a backyard setting. One day out in the sun isn't going to destroy most sofas or tables, and lounging on proper furniture al fresco is spectacular.

sign it up

No matter how scrupulous you've been about designing the flow of your party, your guest will walk in with mixed feelings of hesitancy and excitement. You've intrigued them with your invitation, and they don't know exactly what to expect. The best host will do everything she can to orient a new arrival and give her guests a sense of guidance throughout the party. Some of this is done in person, of course. You greet your guest. You take his coat. You offer her a drink. But you can do more.

Signage is a beautiful, inexpensive, and easy way to sustain your guests' feeling of comfort and purpose. By signage I mean menus, labels, and nametags. Let me break it down for you.

FOOD AND DRINKS

Absolutely find a way to tell your guests what exactly they are eating and drinking. Not only is signage hospitable, but it is an excellent flourish. Your guests will feel like they are in expert hands.

My favorite ways to present menus to guests are via chalkboards and frames. Chalkboard menus have a relaxed, French-restaurant feel to them. Using chalkboard paint, you can be creative and surprising. Paint a large piece of plywood and lean it against the wall behind your dessert table. Suddenly your dessert table is much more dramatic. Paint small pieces of plywood and prop them up against a wall, set them on inexpensive easels, or drill holes in them and hang them in place of your existing artwork. (Yes, you can do this. It's as easy as hanging a picture on the wall.) Picture frames

Vanilla Panna Cotta

are perfect for food or drink menus. Buy inexpensive ones or temporarily repurpose the ones you already have in your house. A punch bowl is a beautiful centerpiece for a drink table. But nobody wants to imbibe a mystery drink. Describe what it is: "Rose champagne punch with fresh raspberries" in a simple frame, and suddenly it's deliciously appealing.

{trainwreck}
SIGNAGE TYPO

The more signs you make, the more chances there are for error. My worst typo was at a dinner party I threw for a friend's mother. There was a menu at every plate, and at the top of the menu I put what I thought was the guest of honor's last name. It *was* my friend's last name, but it was also the name of his mother's ex-husband—a name she had dropped like a hot potato in the divorce. I only realized the error as the guests were already coming to their seats. What could I do? I grabbed my friend James and we snatched the menus off the plates. I grabbed one of our flower displays and attempted to sprinkle petals from the flowers on each plate to compensate for the missing menus, which made me look disorganized and silly as the guests filtered in. I should have just let it go.

{tori TIP... CONFIRM NAMES. PEOPLE ARE SENSITIVE ABOUT THEM. AND WHEN SOMETHING GOES WRONG IN THE MIDDLE OF A PARTY, DO YOUR BEST TO CLEAN UP THE MESS, BUT DON'T BOTHER MAKING A SUBSTITUTION UNLESS IT'S A CRITICAL SITUATION.

TAGS

I am a huge fan of tags. They take any party to another level. Imagine that you have made pulled pork sandwiches for a casual lunch. Now wrap each one in butcher paper and make a sticker tag for it. Stack them in a sideways basket and suddenly your simple baguettes are a gourmet treat. Make favors for a garden party by filling small mason jars with special jam and affixing a handmade tag with baker's twine. How delightful is it to see a row of favor bags and find the one that someone has carefully labeled with your own name? Or as you leave you are handed a homemade cookie wrapped in cellophane, tied with a ribbon and a tag. The perfect favor.

Make your own cool printed tags and labels by hand or online. Ideally, all signage should match, starting with the invitation. The tags on the alcohol should match the nametags for dinner should match the favor bag nametags. If time runs short, have your kids handwrite and decorate labels for everything. It makes them part of the party, and imperfection is cute when it comes from the hands of a child.

I have to confess that I'm not entirely satisfied with the tag-making options out there. When I went to my local craft store for cool hole punchers, all they had were stupid clovers and hearts. Label makers are too overwhelming. For now, until something better comes along, I settle for printing my tags on nice paper and trimming the edges with craft scissors to make the edges zigzag or scalloped. I punch a hole and use baker's twine (which comes in all colors) or grosgrain to attach the tag.

what's on the surface matters

I never thought about this until I started throwing lots of parties, but much of what I design takes place on flat surfaces. Think about it. Parties are about serving, and serving is done on tables and trays. Now I'm going to talk about how to make those flat surfaces spring to life with color and dimension.

TABLETOPS

Start by giving all of your tabletops matching or coordinating bases. Welcome to the wonderful world of fabric. You can buy the cheapest table in the universe for six bucks at a garage sale, drape it in the same interesting fabric as your dining table, and nobody will know the difference in quality. There is a massive range in price for available fabric. Work within your means by going to sales at fabric stores, scouting at garage sales, and making use of unexpected cloth you might have at home.

For even more inexpensive options, use chalkboard paint to create a sleek slate top that doubles as a way to label your dishes. Or cover the table in burlap that you tie down with twine or ribbon. Another option is to layer dark paper over light paper and use a hole puncher to cut flowers (or anything else) out of the dark layer. If it's a glass-top table, shine a light from below to make the flowers glow. Or cut out the name of the guest of honor on the top layer.

Once you have a nice base, dress up your table. You don't even have to cover the table if you plan to decorate the top with flowers and candles. And don't forget the food, which is a design element, too. Think of food that

fits your concept, and garnish it with the colors you've picked. (I'll talk about this more specifically in the Food section.)

As an example, for a shabby chic birthday, I glued fabric and bits of lace to some trays, and spread doilies on others. I like to spray paint the doilies to make them gold, Tiffany blue, or blush. Pick garden roses or some of the cheaper ones from the florist and cluster them on one side of the tray. Symmetry is nice, but I don't like things to be too matchy-matchy, particularly with a rustic, organic theme like shabby chic. Surround the trays of food with clusters of candles, then use frames and flowers to fill the table out completely.

For a Marie Antoinette wedding that was all about opulence, I went downtown and bought cheap cameos, brooches, and buttons. I threaded them onto ribbons, bunched them into cornucopias on the tables, and wove them around candelabras and flowers. It was the picture of opulence, but up close it was just clusters of simple, inexpensive sundries.

For a mod effect, you could paint a table with a high-shine black or red lacquer and cover it with palm fronds or banana leaves. Or transform your tables into Mondrian-style line art by using happytape, colored masking tape from Japan that comes in all different colors. Cut your food into squares and serve it on bamboo disposable plates, preferably square as well.

CUSTOM TRAYS

Trays are a beautiful way to serve food, whether you're passing them around the party or just using them to create color on a simply dressed table. I use the same three trays at every single party I throw. I just spray paint them with lacquer to match the flowers. It's about the details.

For a pug-themed wedding I threw, I took those same trays, glued pictures of pugs onto them, and decoupaged the whole thing. As the hors d'oeuvres were eaten, the pictures of pugs were revealed.

You can paint that same tray with chalkboard paint and write a description of what you're serving right next to the food.

Another simple, elegant approach is to create a floral border with extra stems from your arrangements. If you want a more attention-grabbing floral tray, put gardeners' foam on top of the tray, crowd carnation blossoms with uniformly cut short stems into the foam until they cover it completely, and settle a group of cupcakes on top of your beautiful flowerbed.

DECOUPAGE
{how-to}

If you've never decoupaged before, don't be scared. It's not as fancy as it sounds. If you graduated from kindergarten, you've got all the skills you need. You are basically just cutting out pictures and gluing them onto a surface.

1. Pick your surface. You can decoupage anything from wood, to bottles, to garbage cans, to wine bottles (which make nice candleholders).

2. Cut out the pictures you plan to use. You can choose photos, labels, post-cards . . . anything that works for your concept.

3. Glue the pictures onto the surface.

4. Paint over the whole collage with diluted white glue. There are special decoupage glues out there, but regular school glue works just fine.

5. Let your work dry, then paint it again. About three to four layers of glue should do the trick.

Now your collage is transformed into a shiny, finished surface. So crafty!

FABRIC TRAY
{how-to}

For a simple, shabby chic tray, use a picture frame and fabric to create a simple, beautiful effect.

1. Find old frames—I like distressed ones best.

2. At Home Depot, request plywood cut to the proper size for your frames.

3. Wrap the wood in fabric, staple gun the fabric to the wood, and slide it into the frame.

GO VERTICAL

The food and beverages demand that you pay attention to horizontal surfaces. For exactly that reason, it creates immediate dramatic flare if you have vertical lines to keep your guests' eyes moving around the room. On the buffet tables themselves, create height by hiding stacks of books under the tablecloth, allowing you to place food at different levels. This can be interesting on any table but it is critical on the dessert table! And don't forget the ever-chic tiered servers and pedestal cake plates (which can be stacked for even more drama).

Consider hanging lights or flowers above your food and drink. The tissue paper flower balls I did for the Guncles' baby shower were simple to make and worked wonders to transform the dessert table into a discrete space. You can also, as I've mentioned, create a backdrop for your serving table to set it off from the room as a whole. An easy way to do this is with a color-coordinated sheet or piece of fabric. It is slightly more labor to paint a piece of plywood in the perfect color, but (as with the trays) you can repaint that piece of plywood for party after party.

And for the final touch to your vertical elements, definitely wear heels. Your own magnificent height is essential.

TULLE BALLS
{how-to}

1. Cut a piece of cardboard into a bagel shape. For a small tulle ball, try a diameter of twelve inches, for large, use a diameter of thirty inches, but any sizing will work and I encourage you to mix it up. Make the inside hole big enough for your hand to fit through. Now make another bagel exactly the same size.

2. Cut a piece of string, twine, or ribbon, and make it into a U. Sandwich it between the two bagel sides so that the U goes around the inner hole. You're going to use this ribbon to secure the tulle.

3. Cut one to three yards of tulle. (One for a small ball; three for a big one.) Take one end and wrap it around and around the cardboard, through the middle hole, until the cardboard is entirely covered with a layer of tulle.

4. Now cut the tulle all the way around the circumference of the bagel. Don't cut that middle ribbon.

5. Peek into the middle of your bagel and grab the ribbon. Tie it tightly.

6. Now pull the cardboard off your ball, fluff it up, and . . . gorgeous! Hang multiples from the ceiling, put them in bowls, or use them to embellish serving trays. Love your craftiness!

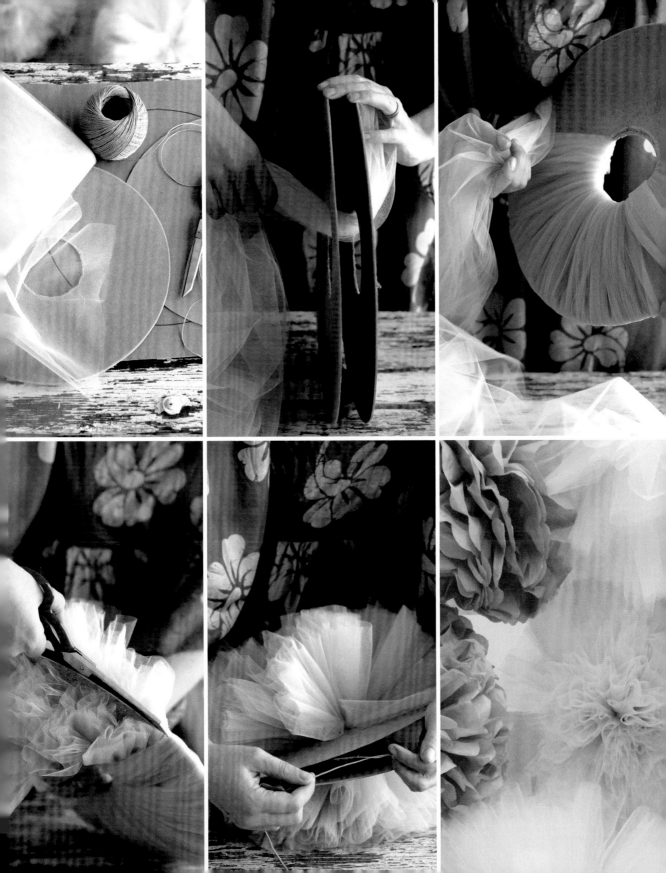

the magic glow

Lighting serves a purpose, of course. Indoors or out, it is critical that your party be lit well enough for even the tipsiest of your guests to see who they are talking to, what they are eating, and where they are walking. And yet as every woman who has ever stepped into the unforgiving fluorescent lights of an elevator or a dressing room knows, it should not be so well lit as to be unflattering. I don't care how swank and modern and dimmable recessed lighting is—it is not appropriate for a party. It shines straight down on top of your head. Ugh. All lighting should be indirect. That means it should never, ever shine in the direction of a person. A candle that flickers toward the ceiling? Yes. A table lamp that sheds a soft, low-wattage light into its shade? Sure. No. Overhead. Lights.

Use general lighting to set boundaries. If you don't want guests in a room, keep it dark and close the door. Just like at the theater, where only the stage is lit, the party is the center of the action. All the guests should be drawn to the world that you've created for tonight.

Focus most of your effort on lighting the food and beverage tables. If the food can be seen and your space isn't enormous, that should be enough wattage to carry the rest of the party. Candles are easy, beautiful, and inexpensive. Buy a bunch of reasonably priced tea candles and glass votive holders. You'll use them at every party until the end of time. Or, if you have an assortment of interesting drinking glasses, put candles in them and cluster those instead. This is a great example of where mismatching adds appeal. Oh, and make sure the candles are unscented, please, people. One lightly scented candle is acceptable in the bathroom, but no more!

{more about}
MISMATCHING

When you have multiples of some piece of décor, be it votives, frames, pillows, or scarves, don't be afraid to use them as a mismatched group. All items shouldn't be identical, or the décor will look factory-generic. Here's a simple rule of thumb. In a grouping, every item should be different, but there should be *something* that unifies them. All frames are silver, but they're different shapes. All votives are glass, with a lace ribbon tied around them, but they are different heights. All single-stem flowers are in your grandmother's old, mismatched teacups. Don't take it too far, though. Your favor bags may have different colored tags or ribbons, but the effect should be that they are all nearly identical, clustered in a lovely basket or lined up like elegant soldiers, ready for the charge.

CHINESE LANTERNS

When you need more lighting than you have—which most often happens at an outside party—my favorite choice is round Chinese lanterns. They're inexpensive, they come in every color and size imaginable, and they have a clean, modern look. They couldn't be easier to string up. Chic and functional—what could be better?

favors

Every party should have some kind of takeaway. I learned this from my mother, and it's important. You're not only saying thank you to your guests for attending, but in a small but real way you're reminding them that they are an important presence in your life. You wanted them there. They came. You tried to create a unique experience for them. Even if you didn't get to talk to them, you hope they had a nice time and that this token will sustain the mood that your party created for a little bit longer as they reenter their lives.

If your budget is small, it's easy to make a modest favor. My go-to choice is a cookie that is shaped and decorated according to my concept. I've also given a candle, or wildflowers wrapped in twine in my color scheme. Have fun with favors. If you have a martini party, give guests a mason jar with homemade stuffed olives. Wrap the top with twine and a handmade tag.

The most important element of the favor is the packaging and the presentation. The favors must match. They must serve your concept. They

don't have to be fancy or expensive. Cleverness and beauty is much more important than fanciness. Decorating the bag can be a kid-friendly project. You can get simple white gift bags at Target and use rubber letter stamps to spell out your guests' names. Or use stickers. In the course of the party the cluster of beautiful favor bags lined up or otherwise displayed will be a dramatic, compelling part of the décor.

We have covered all the critical aspects of party décor—except the one so important it deserves its own section. Flowers.

part four:
FLOWERS

Flowers are a beautiful element to add to any party. But please remember that you aren't planning a wedding. Gigantic, over-the-top centerpieces are inappropriate in a home, where there aren't so many tables. Flowers should be used strictly for accents. They welcome guests in the entry hallway or near the door. They attract attention to the bar, the food, and the dessert table. They add a pop of color and freshness to the powder room.

the flower market

The florists of America are going to kill me for this, but one of my best budget tips is to ban the florist. Instead, shop where the florists shop: at the closest flower market or farmers' market. If you live in a more rural locale, you can even order flowers online, setting the day before the party as your delivery date.

Don't be intimidated by the idea of taking the flowers into your own hands. You can do it. Anyone can walk into flower markets. You may have to pay a dollar or so to enter, but that's it. Go early in the morning on the day before your party. The prices will amaze you. One hydrangea stem will cost a dollar or so, whereas the florist would charge you at least five dollars for the same flower. You can fully deck out a small house party—I'm talking over-the-top floral madness that would cost a thousand dollars from a florist—for a hundred dollars.

style

Keep your floral elements chic and refined. Pick one color from your concept and work within that color, with varying shades or types of flower. Even on a small scale, don't feel like you need to create complex arrangements. I love to put single stems in votives and to create small clusters of them at key points. Dahlias or peonies are beautiful alone. This is the cheapest and best way of turning a surface into something special.

containers

There's no need to buy fifteen vases. Anything can serve as a votive. You can use regular cups, glass cups, vintage teacups, a decanter—any simple jars or other glassware. The stuff around your house can be much nicer than plain old glass vases. Or you can make it so. If you want to be more creative, wrap the glassware in fabric, wrapping paper, leaves, or lace. Tie a ribbon around it.

GIVE CARNATIONS
a chance

The poor maligned carnation. Carnations have a bad rap. They are cheap and often badly dyed. Sure, green Saint Patrick's Day carnations are a turnoff. But there is more to them than that. I want to single-handedly start a carnation renaissance. They are an amazing filler flower. They come in all colors and look beautiful in an arrangement. They are hardy, full, and pretty. I especially love to use them in flower balls. Half the time someone will come up to me and ask what kind of flower I used. When I tell them it's a carnation, they are shocked.

Roses are red
Violets are blue
Carnations are amazing
You should use them, too.

Intricate, multiflower arrangements can be a little overwhelming. If you want to create larger arrangements, I suggest you stick to a single kind of flower. Use all peonies, all hydrangeas, or all roses. It's so easy and creates a more contemporary look. I happen to prefer low arrangements. They're pretty, and if you have room you can use them on tables without blocking the view of the food.

THINKING OUTSIDE THE VASE

I encourage you to think beyond flowers. What else could you put in a vase? Mix burgundy dahlias with unusual fruits in the same shades. Or skip the flowers altogether and display cut pomegranates and cut figs, which look beautiful displayed in bowls. Even familiar, everyday items acquire new beauty and meaning when grouped into displays. For my back-to-school party, I filled tall glass jars with crayons, erasers, pencils, and rubber bands. These décor elements function exactly like flowers—they add spots of color and festivity throughout your space.

Your flowers do double duty if you use them as favors. For the favor at my own baby shower, I had a make-your-own-bouquet station. It was set up in a big, old-fashioned flower cart. (Over-the-top, I know, but you could use a plain old wheelbarrow if you're a wheelbarrow-owning household, or a galvanized tin that you might otherwise use for drinks on ice.) Inside the flower cart, the flowers were in aluminum buckets, prettily labeled, of course. Everyone picked their flowers, wrapped them in precut brown paper, and tied it with raffia. It was beautiful during the party, and afterward everyone went home with a bouquet of their own design.

{trainwreck}

FLOWER POWER TURNS SOUR

When I threw a baby shower for the Guncles' new baby Simone, I ordered one hundred raspberry dahlias, which I stored in buckets (as you always should) over the weekend. Never mind the logistics, but the buckets of flowers were at the production office for my show. Unbeknownst to me, the air conditioning in the office went out. It was a typically hot August weekend. When I went to pick up the dahlias, they were all sad and wilted. Almost unusable. Almost. I had no other options, so I propped them up in tight bunches so their droopy heads stood a little bit taller and placed them around the party.

Setup for that party took far longer than I anticipated. Liam and Stella had helped me make raspberry tissue paper flowers that I wanted to hang from the ceiling. When the guests arrived, I was still on a ladder trying to get those damned flowers to hang right. My friend Chris was still putting the cookies out on trays. I had to tell Bill and Scout to wait downstairs with the baby while we finished.

{tori TIP... TAKE IT FROM ME. LEAVE NOTHING EXCEPT HOT FOOD AND ICE FOR THE DAY OF THE PARTY. BUT TREAT YOUR FLOWERS WITH THE UTMOST OF CARE.

Beautiful as flowers are, in most of my parties they are usually peripheral. They are pretty surprises that fill out tables, add color and scent, and pull a room together. Now it's time to get to the heart of the party—the food and drink.

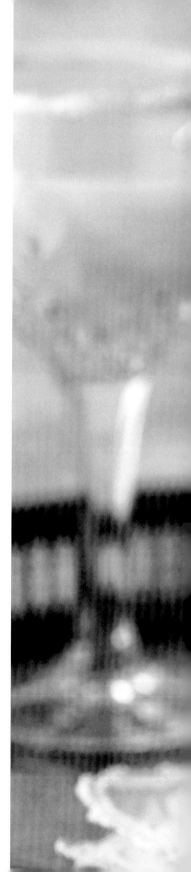

part five:

FOOD AND DRINK

A party is more than a space that you create for people to gather for celebration and conversation. There's a reason for the expression "Eat, drink, and make merry." Without the first two, it's hard to do the third.

drink basics

Your drink offerings should include water, something nonalcoholic, a specialized cocktail or two, and wine. You can also add a basic bar if you want to provide more options.

REFRESHMENT

I hate water. It's just so . . . hydrating. Form over function, right? Instead I offer sparkling water at my parties. I like to experiment with adding fruits and herbs to it. I'll take strawberries and basil and muddle them into sparkling water, put it in a punch bowl or a pitcher with some whole strawberries and leaves floating on the top, and it's a delicious, pretty, nonalcoholic option. For plain water, which apparently many people expect and enjoy, please at the very least put it in a glass pitcher with some ice and lemon.

I like to include soda at all parties and beer at daytime or casual evening parties. Jones Soda Co. makes many flavors of soda, from bubble gum to cream soda, and the bottles come in awesome colors to match almost any color scheme. The bottles have a cute label, and on their website you can even customize the label with a photo. For Liam's baby shower I used blue Jones Soda bottles as the invitations. Over the regular label I put a new label that I had created with all the invitation details. It was fabulous.

dean's favorite gingerade

....

1. Fill bar shaker with ice. Add lemonade, honey syrup, and ginger concentrate.

2. Shake.

3. Pour into glass and top off with 2 ounces soda water and 3 dashes of bitters.

1 cup lemonade

1½ ounces honey syrup*

¾ ounce ginger concentrate**

*HONEY SYRUP (FOR GINGERADE)

1. Add equal amounts of honey and water.

2. Bring to boil in pot.

3. Let cool and use.

**GINGER CONCENTRATE (FOR GINGERADE)

1. Coarsely shred a good hunk of ginger.

2. Add to 1½ cups water.

3. Bring to boil in pot.

4. Let simmer for 20–30 minutes.

5. Strain through tea strainer or cheesecloth.

6. Let cool and use.

SPECIALTY COCKTAILS

Nothing makes a party like a signature drink. As people arrive, getting a drink gives them something to do. Having it in hand makes them comfortable. It helps them unwind. The cocktail choices that you invent are a natural conversation springboard for guests who have never met before. "What's this? A *Pucci-tini*? Have you tasted it yet?"

I like to have two premade signature cocktails. Generally, I provide a foofy drink—something sweet and colorful—and a more hardcore drink, like a gin and tonic or a dirty martini. Of course you must factor in what your guest of honor would like best.

Your specialty cocktails don't have to be alcoholic—in fact it's nice to give guests the option to abstain or to pace themselves—but it is mandatory that drinks have names and accompanying signage, of course. Name them after your guest of honor, or the occasion, or the party mascot. When creativity fails you, end the name with -tini. For my Marie Antoinette party, we served a Let Them Eat Cake Martini, which was a vanilla martini served in a glass that was rimmed with white icing dipped in blush pink sugar crystals. For baby Simone's shower, I served Simply Simone Sangria, which was a rose sangria garnished with all red and pink berries. For a pug party, I made a Pug-itini. It was just a variation on a martini, but the name gave it character. The point is to serve drinks that are unique and special to the occasion. It's about creating a memory as much as a buzz.

{trainwreck}

WHEN A GUEST IS OVERSERVED

The most common party foul is a guest who has had one too many of those fabulous signature cocktails you concocted. We all have our moments. One of my most egregious happened to take place at my former costar Jason Priestley's engagement party. Youth wasn't my excuse—this happened when I was thirty-one years old. I don't know what went wrong that night, but I ended up so wasted that I was sick in Jason's bathroom. This was not a large, rollicking party where such behavior, if not appropriate, might at least go unnoticed. There were only about twenty civilized adults in attendance, all of whom were very aware of my embarrassing situation.

I woke up the next day and my first thought was, "Really? *That* happened?" Their wedding was rapidly approaching, and I waited patiently for them to tell me that the wedding was off—they were going to elope—or that my invitation was lost in the mail. But they must have forgiven me because my invitation arrived, and I went to the wedding, where I made sure to conduct myself like a lady.

Often (and in that case) when a guest is overserved, I place at least some of the blame on the server. When a server refills glasses or brings new drinks around on a tray, it's all too easy for guests to help themselves to another drink. And another. They lose track of how much they've had. And they don't circulate as much. They get stuck in one place, in one conversation, while the drinks keep flowing. I prefer to have a bar, where the guests need to make an effort and a choice to have another. If you do hire servers, make sure they don't overdo it. Tell them to keep an eye on guests and to rein it in. (Okay, fine, I guess I have to take responsibility for my own overconsumption. But it was an honest mistake.)

If someone does drink too much at your party, you must manage the situation with grace. Tempting as it is to stick a lampshade on your guest's head and take pictures for future extortion opportunities, it is your job as a host to get your guest home safely and discreetly. Do not ask if your guest needs a ride—duh, his judgment is impaired. Simply arrange one and escort him to it, favor in hand, as if this were the plan all along.

Some people really hate to leave their cars behind. If this is the case, simply have someone drive his car and send along a follow car. Who doesn't love to do a good deed? If at all possible, choose two single people who are a possible match to do this. Their drive back to your house together will be a perfect get-to-know-you moment.

{tori TIP... SACRIFICE GRACE TO SAVE A LIFE. IF YOU'RE TIMID, LIKE ME, ENLIST YOUR PUSHIEST FRIEND.

let them eat cake martini

Vanilla icing

Sanding sugar, blush or light pink

2 ounces vanilla vodka

1 ounce pineapple juice

1 ounce cranberry juice

1–1½ teaspoons agave nectar
  (sweeten to your taste)

½ ounce half & half

Optional: ½ ounce almond
  liqueur or ½ ounce amaretto

1. Ice the rim of a martini glass with vanilla icing and dust with blush or light pink sanding sugar.

2. Combine all other ingredients in a shaker with ice. Shake well. Strain into the martini glass. Top it off with a cocktail pick skewering a small piece of angel food cake iced with white frosting.

ginger margarita

1. In a saucepan, make simple syrup by bringing the water and sugar to a light simmer. Cook until sugar is dissolved.

2. Add ginger and steep for 30 minutes.

3. Pour ginger and simple syrup into a blender and puree.

4. Strain out pulp. This puree can be stored in a tightly sealed bottle or jar for up to 3 weeks in the refrigerator.

5. When you're ready, add tequila and lime juice to 5 ounces of the ginger simple syrup puree and ice into a shaker. Shake well. Yields four drinks.

1½ cups water

¾ cup sugar

1 large "hand" of ginger, peeled and cut into ½-inch chunks

2 ounces tequila, per drink

Juice of 1 lime, plus some lime wedges for garnish

Sanding sugar (for glass)

Freshly grated nutmeg

DRESS THE GLASS:

1. On a plate, pour some sanding sugar and grate a pinch of nutmeg into it. Mix.

2. Run a lime wedge around the rim of the glass.

3. Dip rim of glass into the sanding sugar. Rotate glass to coat rim.

4. Add the contents of the shaker into the glass, straining out the ice.

Optional: Grate a little bit of nutmeg on top and serve with a lime.

{ moneysaver }

DO-IT-YOURSELF CHAMPAGNE/VODKA BAR

For a last-minute cocktail party with a girly group—of boys—I decided to create a do-it-yourself champagne/vodka bar. Those two alcohols covered the bases: champagne for those who wanted something light, vodka for those who liked a stiffer drink. And the do-it-yourself factor meant that I wouldn't have to hire a bartender or mix drinks myself. Making a drink would be a fun party activity and, I hoped, an icebreaker. In addition to the two alcohol bases, I also provided soda, cassis, and cranberry juice. All the base drinks went in decanters. Then, into tall, old-fashioned, glass bottles with pour stoppers, I decanted all sorts of flavored syrups: elderflower, watermelon, pomegranate, blood orange, etc. I set out garnishes: berries, pomegranate seeds, orange rind, lemon peel, basil, rosemary. I handmade tags for the drinks, the syrups, and the garnishes. When

I was done it looked beautiful. At the party, however, I was disappointed to see that the guests seemed frozen at the table. They weren't sure what to mix. When I came up and said, "Try the champagne with a hint of elderberry and a sprig of mint," they thawed a little, mixed it up, and were happy with the results. But I couldn't stand there making drink recommendations all night. The whole idea was to save money on a bartender, not to become one myself! I still love the concept, and I suffered for your benefit. Now we know that guests need signs suggesting possible mixes. By assigning the labels categories (a round label for garnishes, a rectangular label for syrups, a square label for juices, etc.), I showed my guests that they could make a lovely drink by picking one from each category.

Start with Vodka or Champagne & add a

Splash of Juice

Touch of Liqueur

Hint of Flavor

+ Garnish =

Your Perfect Combination

food basics

Feasting guests are happy guests. You must tend to all your guests' senses, and taste is an important one. You can't serve your guests prefab party plates and think they're going to have a spectacular evening. But that doesn't mean you have to prepare a five-course gourmet meal. In fact, I rarely host sit-down dinner parties. I prefer a buffet, which is more casual and allows guests to mingle freely, to eat at their own pace, and to arrive at and leave the party on their own schedules. And nobody gets stuck talking endlessly to the people they happen to be sitting near. When I do have dinner parties, I still let the guests serve themselves at a buffet or pass dishes family-style.

FEED YOUR FRIENDS

My mother and Jenny taught me long ago that if you call a party for a certain time, you must serve dinner or heavy, heavy hors d'oeuvres. I once went to an eight o'clock party on an empty stomach where the only food available was three appetizers that a waiter occasionally brought into my vicinity: goat cheese tartlets, bruschetta, and asparagus wrapped in prosciutto. This was dinner? The company was nice, but eventually my stomach was growling so loudly that I could barely make conversation. Dean and I went to In-N-Out Burger on the way home.

It can be tough to judge quantity, but you must always do as I do: err on the side of making too much food. Better to have leftovers than hungry guests. Although I've learned that I go overboard every single time, I don't seem to be able to change. Nonetheless, my advice is to come up with a list of all the dishes you'd like to make, then pare it down. For a midsize party

I like to make several appetizers, two main dishes (one of which is vegetarian), and a couple side dishes. I scale up or down depending on the size of the party or if I want it to be appetizer- or dinner-heavy.

Budget your time and be realistic about what you can pull off. If your dishes include tried-and-true, easy-to-make food, like crudités or a cheese plate, then you can afford to be more ambitious with the other dishes.

One simple way to up the ante is to go all out with your cheese plate, with big wheels of elegant cheese hand-tagged like at an elegant cheese store. An elaborate cheese plate is an excellent opportunity for signage. It's a no-brainer. You can have cheeses handpicked to pair with quince, sliced figs, fresh fruit, olives, and nuts. You can even add meats or a whole charcuterie board. For one party I made several small charcuterie boards for two to three people to indulgently share with hard cheese, soft cheese, olives, nuts, sausage, and prosciutto. Without fail, cheese is always a huge hit.

Any cheese tastes better when it's sliced. Even at kids' parties I'll put

{trainwreck}
RUNNING OUT OF FOOD

I make way too much food. It's just my nature. But one time I hosted a tea party—it was at three o'clock so I just made mini sandwiches. Dessert was Bananas Foster, which I planned to bring out, flaming of course, later in the party. Within five minutes, all of the mini sandwiches were gone. I'd made about four tea sandwiches per person, which I thought added up to a whole sandwich each, but for some reason people were really hungry that day. The arrival of the dessert was supposed to be an event in itself. The grand finale. But with an empty food table, we had no choice. We brought out the Bananas Foster.

{tori TIP... NEVER SCRIMP ON DESSERT. WHEN ALL ELSE FAILS, IT WILL SAVE YOU.

out a bowl of Babybel cheese, sliced, and the adults can't get enough of it.

For buffets and parties where you're only serving hors d'oeuvres, it's best to choose dishes that work at room temperature. You can prepare them further in advance and you'll save yourself from worrying if the food has gone cold and running back and forth to the kitchen to heat another batch.

BRING ON THE YUMMY

A buffet should be full of delicious food, calorie content be damned. It's a party, not a wellness retreat. I mean, if I'm hosting an afternoon party, I do feel obligated to put out a salad. I feel like people expect something light and healthy in the middle of the day. Nobody really eats it, but everyone feels better. Otherwise, keep it simple and delicious, and stick to what you know.

A party is not the best venue for risky experimentation. Keep it simple. For the most part, if a kid likes it, it will be a hit at a party. Mac and cheese, grilled cheese with tomato soup shots, taquitos, cocktail weenies, even mini peanut butter and jelly sandwiches. I've been serving the same frozen mini quiches that I buy at Costco since I first started hosting parties. Nobody ever pooh-poohs them. They are a stand-up app. Say what you want, but I guarantee that if you place any of these options next to some schmancy smoked salmon, the kid-inspired food plate will be clean long before the gourmet salmon apps have been touched. It's good to be adventurous, just don't do it at the cost of your other dishes. Save the preparation of your adventurous dish for last, or take the time to practice in advance. Or reinvent something you know. Try making gourmet pizzas on premade crusts: one savory (cheeses with meats or vegetables) and one sweet (fig jam, goat cheese, and sliced fig). Or take a traditionally hearty dish that you've made in the past as a main course, like chili or steak sandwiches, and offer it in mini form.

baked brie and jam 'n puff pastry

This is a simple recipe that takes serving cheese up a level. It's one of my party staples.

1. Preheat oven to 350°.

2. In small bowl mix the jam and jelly together.

3. Coat top of Brie wheel with jam mixture (add chopped nuts if desired).

4. Place pastry sheet on top of Brie wheel and wrap, folding excess pastry underneath. If too much dough, cut it down.

5. Grease a cookie sheet, place in center of oven, and bake 25 to 30 minutes. Watch that dough doesn't get too brown.

6. Allow to cool 5 minutes, then serve with crackers.

¼ cup seedless raspberry jam

¼ cup jalapeño jelly

1 round Brie

1 large sheet frozen puff pastry dough or 1 tube of refrigerated crescent dinner rolls, thawed

Optional: chopped walnuts or pecans

swedish meatballs with lingonberry sauce

1 cup fresh bread crumbs, dried out

¾ cup milk

6 tablespoons unsalted butter

4 shallots, minced

2 garlic cloves, minced

1 teaspoon caraway seeds, toasted and ground

1 pound ground beef

1 pound ground pork

1 egg

½ handful of fresh flat leaf parsley, chopped

1 handful fresh dill, chopped

Salt and fresh-ground white pepper to taste

2 tablespoons all-purpose flour

1½ cups chicken broth

¾ cup sour cream

¼ cup lingonberry (IKEA sells it!) or red currant jam (plus more for serving)

1. In a bowl, combine bread crumbs and milk. Stir with a fork and let stand for 5 minutes.

2. Put 3 tablespoons butter in a small skillet and let it melt over medium heat.

3. Add shallots, garlic, and caraway seeds to skillet and season with salt and pepper. Cook until softened but not brown, for approximately 2 minutes.

4. Put ground beef and pork in a large bowl. Add the shallot mixture, egg, parsley, and dill. Season with salt and pepper.

5. Squeeze milk out of soaked bread crumbs and add the bread to the meat mixture. Mix it all well using your hands.

6. Pinch off a chunk of the meat mixture and roll it in the palm of your hands to shape it into a ball about the size of a ping-pong ball.

7. Form the rest of the meat mixture into balls and set them aside.

8. Melt 2 tablespoons of the butter in a large skillet over moderate heat. When the foam starts to go away, add the meatballs in small batches so you don't over-crowd the skillet.

9. Sauté meatballs until browned evenly for approximately 5 to 6 minutes. Remove the meatballs onto a paper towel–lined platter.

10. Throw away most of the fat from the skillet and return to heat.

11. Add remaining tablespoon of butter and make sure it coats the whole skillet.

12. Sprinkle in the flour and stir with a wooden spoon to dissolve into fat.

13. Pour in chicken broth and stir with the wooden spoon. Stir and simmer until liquid is reduced and a sauce starts to form. Season with salt and pepper.

14. Lower heat and stir in sour cream.

15. Return meatballs to the sauce and stir in ¼ cup lingonberry jam until combined.

16. Simmer until sauce thickens slightly and meatballs are heated throughout.

17. Serve with toothpicks, on a mini spoon, or pierced with a mini fork.

18. Serve lingonberry jam on the side as a dip if desired.

t's meaty lasagna

Olive oil, for sautéing and pasta water

½ cup minced onion

2 cloves garlic, crushed

1 pound ground beef

1 pound sweet Italian sausage

1 can (28 ounces) stewed or
    crushed tomatoes

2 cans (6 ounces) tomato paste

2 cans (6 ounces) tomato sauce

½ cup water

2 tablespoons white sugar

1½ tablespoons dried parsley

1½ tablespoons dried basil

1 tablespoon salt

1 teaspoon Italian seasoning

¼ teaspoon ground black pepper

1 teaspoon dried oregano

1 package lasagna noodles

½ teaspoon salt, to add to pasta
    water

16 ounces ricotta cheese

2 whole eggs, beaten

2 tablespoons finely chopped fresh
    Italian parsley

½ cup grated Parmesan cheese

½ teaspoon salt

Approximately 2 eight-ounce packs
    of shredded mozzarella cheese

PREPARE SAUCE:

1. Use 1 tablespoon olive oil to coat a large skillet. Add onions and garlic and stir until they are soft and translucent. Add ground beef and sausage. Combine and cook over medium heat until onions are browned.

2. Pour meat mixture into a large saucepan over medium heat. Add the tomatoes (with their juice), tomato paste, tomato sauce, water, white sugar, dried parsley, dried basil, salt, Italian seasoning, pepper, and dried oregano, or to your taste. Sometimes I add Lawry's seasoned salt instead of salt. Be a scientist and experiment with your sauce!

3. Let the sauce simmer covered, and stir occasionally for approximately 1½ hours or until thickened.

PREPARE NOODLES:

Bring a large pot of lightly salted water to a boil. Add a few drops of olive oil. Add lasagna noodles and cook in boiling water for 8 to 10 minutes. You want the noodles slightly undercooked. Drain the noodles and rinse in cold water.

*celebra*TORI

PREPARE CHEESE MIXTURE:

While meat/tomato mixture is simmering, in a mixing bowl combine ricotta with beaten eggs. Then add fresh chopped parsley, grated Parmesan cheese, and salt. Stir together and set aside.

ASSEMBLE:

1. Spread 1½ cups of meat sauce in the bottom of a 9x13-inch baking dish.

2. Arrange six noodles, overlapping lengthwise over meat sauce.

3. Spread with half the ricotta cheese mixture. Sprinkle lightly with shredded mozzarella.

4. Spoon 1½ cups of meat sauce over mozzarella.

5. Add another layer of lasagna noodles and repeat steps until your lasagna has reached just below the top of the dish. End on a meat sauce layer.

6. Cover the whole top layer with remaining mozzarella cheese and sprinkle extra grated Parmesan cheese over the top.

BAKE:

1. Spray foil with cooking spray (to prevent cheese sticking to it) and cover lasagna.

2. Bake at 375° for 25 minutes.

3. Remove the foil and bake another 25 minutes or until top is lightly browned, and bubbly but not burned.

4. Cool for 15 minutes before serving.

5. Serve with a great glass of Chianti!

shepherd's pie

1 to 1½ pounds ground
  beef (can substitute
  lamb or turkey)

1 small onion, chopped

2 garlic cloves, minced

1 can beef gravy

¼ teaspoon Worcestershire
  sauce

Salt and pepper to taste

1 cup frozen baby green
  peas (you can use fresh
  but I've been eating the
  frozen since I was a
  kid!)

¼ tablespoon butter

2½ cups mashed potatoes

INGREDIENTS FOR MASHED
POTATOES:

3 pounds Yukon gold
  potatoes, peeled and
  quartered lengthwise

1 teaspoon salt

2 tablespoons butter

½ cup milk

1 cup sour cream

Salt and pepper

MAKE MASHED POTATOES:

1. Put potatoes into a saucepan. Add ½ teaspoon salt. Add water until potatoes are completely covered. Bring to a boil, reduce heat and simmer, covered, 15 to 20 minutes, or until soft enough that a fork can easily be poked through them.

2. Melt butter.

3. Drain water from potatoes and put hot potatoes into a bowl. Add melted butter, milk, and sour cream. Using masher, mash potatoes. Then use a strong spoon to mix further, adding more milk if needed to achieve smoother consistency. Add salt and pepper to taste.

MAKE SHEPHERD'S PIE:

4. In a large skillet, cook beef and onion over medium heat until meat is browned.

5. Add garlic to skillet, cook 1 minute, and drain.

6. Stir in the gravy, Worcestershire sauce, and salt and pepper.

7. In a separate saucepan, heat thawed peas with butter and salt.

8. Have handy the mashed potatoes you've made. (Don't forget lots of sour cream so they are creamy! At least that's how I love 'em.)

9. Transfer meat to a 1½-quart baking dish. Layer peas on top of meat.

10. Spread the mashed potatoes over the top.

11. Bake uncovered at 350° for 30 minutes or until heated through.

Optional: To make mini shepherd's pies use mini ramekins.

It's not fancy, but I love to serve ketchup on the side!

If it ain't broke, don't fix it. Lipton onion soup mix, combined with sour cream, is still my favorite dip, hands down. I ate it every day when I was pregnant with Liam and Stella. Can you put it out for respectable company? Absolutely. It's the best. At the end of every party where I serve it, that bowl is licked clean. People love it, and your job as a host is to aim to please. If I want to do a chic version of onion dip, I'll cut the accompanying potatoes myself, then bake or fry them. But if I'm having a Super Bowl party, it's good old Ruffles potato chips all the way. Yum. There's nothing like an old timeless staple.

{bringing back}
THE JELL-O MOLD

My mother used to make beautiful Jell-O molds for her parties. They were always layered—an inch of green Jell-O, made milky with sour cream, then a layer of plain sour cream, then a layer of pineapple Jell-O with chunks of real pineapple, and so on. I grew up with those Jell-O molds, and I worry that my children's generation will grow up having no idea what a Jell-O mold is. This idea haunts me—What if the art of Jell-O molding is lost forever?—and I am therefore obsessed with bringing the Jell-O mold back in style.

My friend James, who is British, doesn't know from Jell-O molds. He is obsessed with trifles. Anytime we try to think of a new dessert to serve, he pushes for trifle: "Every kid in England has it at their birthday parties. It would be so chic if we served it in a cut-glass bowl with layers of clotted cream." For Liam's superhero birthday party he was dying to make one, but I wasn't sold on the idea. I explained to him that people don't eat trifles here in America, and instead I sold him on Jell-O molds. The night before Liam's party James and I stayed up until one in the morning crafting spectacular red-and-blue layered Jell-O molds, full of fresh strawberries and blueberries. They came out perfectly.

The next day as people arrived at the party I kept saying, "Did you see the Jell-O molds? Did you see them?" Everyone feigned appreciation, but nobody touched them. Not a soul. Nobody wanted to be the first to cut into that wiggly-jiggly perfection. Not even the kids. After the party we had to throw it all away. I had to concede to James that trifle couldn't have been less of a hit.

Maybe the world isn't ready for Jell-O molds, but I'm not done trying. And I hope that one day Stella or Liam or Hattie will take up the mantle.

Prepared food from the grocery store is more expensive. But it's acceptable so long as the presentation is nice. I like to buy little premade tart shells as a base. They are super easy to fill with almost anything savory or sweet—from mac and cheese to mushroom quiche to fruit tarts. I'll even take a Ziploc bag, fill it with soft cheese, cut off the corner, and simply swirl cheese into the little cup. Invent ways to make your food look tasty and festive. Top your tartlet with diced pepper, parsley, rosemary, or a sliver of fruit for a dollop of color. Delicious!

EASE OF USE

One important feature of everything you serve is how easy it is to eat. If something is an hors d'oeuvre or a buffet item that people will probably eat while standing up, possibly trying to drink wine at the same time, you must make sure it is bite-size and not-too-sloppy. Innovation is great until everyone is trying to use chopsticks to manage spaghetti with red sauce. How elegant can a party be if everyone looks like a baby without a bib?

PREPARATION

I'm so bad with time management and food, so this is another place where I advise you to do as I say, not as I do. All crafting should be done weeks before. Paper goods should be purchased and set aside. But for the most part your food should be freshly prepared. Shop for everything the day before and prep as much as you can that same day so that by the day of the party you are all ready to go.

When you plan your menu, factor in the potential consequences of trying to do something complicated. Definitely don't attempt Beef Wellington.

You're just going to have to trust me on that one. No Julia Child recipes. And I recommend avoiding anything like popovers or soufflés that might collapse. There are plenty of amazing desserts that can be prepared in advance.

This past summer for the Fourth of July, Scout was having a birthday party. Dean had been in a bike accident and was in the hospital. I planned to visit Dean at the hospital, then stop by Scout's party, then go back to the hospital. I wanted to make something fun and festive to bring to both Scout and Dean. It was more than a hundred degrees out. Ice cream would have been perfect, but of course it would have melted on my journey, so I came up with the cupcake cone.

PRESENTATION

As you work out your menu, be sure to keep your concept in mind. Every dish should be on theme, whether it is in the ethnicity or style of the food or the presentation or all of the above. Go all out. Sure, you want it to taste good, but the display is equally important. If you're offering salad, you can serve it in color-coordinated Chinese take-out boxes with little chopsticks. At a chic cocktail party you can serve something as simple as mini sliders if you serve them with the best china on silver trays. If you're making watermelon soup, use the empty watermelons as serving bowls.

Your serving platters, plates, and utensils can be paper, plastic, or china. It really depends on the party. If disposable plates are in order, look for the cute eco-friendly ones made of bamboo. They have a nice modern look. They cost a little more, but I consider it an investment in my kids' future.

If I'm doing a garden party, I pull out my china, and if I don't have enough, I borrow from friends. Evening calls for glassware. And if you're having a large group, don't write off renting from party companies. It can

(continued on page 121)

{trainwreck}

THE OVERSIZE HORS D'OEUVRE

Size matters. Once I went to a holiday benefit where celebrities gift-wrap toys for charity. For some reason they happened to be serving gigantic appetizers. There were crab cakes and quiches the size of hamburgers, and egg rolls as long as my arm. Every item was a four-bite affair. I was wearing bright red lipstick that I didn't want to mess up. So I worked out a system with my friend Chris, who was at the party with me. He would take a couple bites of an appetizer, then put the last bite back down on the plate, at which point I would delicately finish it off. We joked that people were whispering, "Tori Spelling makes people bite her appetizers so she doesn't have to eat the whole thing." I guess it was kind of true. But at least it wasn't for the skinny.

{tori TIP...

ALL APPETIZERS
SHOULD BE BITE-SIZE
FINGER FOODS.
AND ALWAYS BRING
A LIPSTICK. PERIOD.

CUPCAKE CONE
{how-to}

Here's how to make cute, yummy, stress-free cupcake cones. Best of all, no melting. Make sure you have some sort of plan for how to keep the finished cones standing. I used an upside-down wire basket to display them. You can also just put them in regular glasses.

1. Bake your favorite cake. I like to make a nine-inch red velvet cake. If you're short on time, use a mix from a box. Why not? When the cake is done, let it cool completely.

2. In a bowl, mush the cake with cream cheese or icing. Keep adding the cream cheese until the consistency is moldable, but not gooey. You're going to want to be able to form balls that stick together well.

3. Put the cake/icing mixture in the freezer until it firms up a bit—about an hour. You don't want it too hard, just firm enough, again, that it will be easy to mold.

4. Now roll the mushy cake into balls, press them firmly onto old-fashioned ice-cream cones.

5. Frost with regular icing.

(continued from page 116)

be surprisingly reasonable. Plus, you don't have to wash the glasses at the end of the night. Bonus!

Your serving plates should be full, but not crowded. I like to place bite-size items in well-spaced lines on the plates, a good width apart so that when someone picks one up, they don't have to touch any of the other servings. Don't succumb to the temptation to put out every morsel you've prepared at the start of the party. Replenishing the dishes is more work, but if you don't crowd the food, you can just pop replacements into the missing spaces in your neat rows and the presentation stays fresh and pretty all night long. I'd rather replenish.

Arrange foods that are meant to be eaten together in groups, ideally on a single tray. You don't want to do all the work for your guests—you're not going to prepare the cheese and cracker servings—but do clue people in so they don't wonder if they're getting it right.

MONEY *versus* LABOR

Make, buy, borrow, or rent? Suffer, enlist friends, or hire? I'm a die-hard do-it-myselfer, but I've learned (the hard way) that sometimes it is just plain better, and even sometimes cheaper, to throw money at the problem. Take party rentals. Most people assume that for a small party at home, renting isn't an option. They need more outdoor furniture, so they either go out and buy stuff they don't really need and must find a place to store it afterward; they spend an entire day carting tables from a friend's house; or they try to cobble together a half-assed solution. Even when you're on a tight budget, it's worth investigating the cost of renting furniture, linens, and even glassware in your neighborhood. They might be cheaper than you think. Time is money, people. Weigh your options.

The same is true when it comes to hiring help. If you're willing to hire a babysitter for a night on the town, why wouldn't you hire a bartender for the same price to pour drinks and to keep surfaces clean as the party goes on? Throw a local college student a bone. You'll have more fun, and you won't end up talking to your guests while holding a stack of filthy dishes. Gross.

POTATO BAR

*Mashed
*Skins
*Frites

{ Parm, Blue, Cheddar, Truffle, Chives,
Bacon, Crème Fraîche, Butter }

OVER-THE-TOP SPECIALIZED FOOD STATIONS

Now, if you're ready for the big leagues, you can take your food to the next level with a specialized food station. Start with one basic, popular food, and give your guests several ways in which to customize it. My potato bar had three different items: French fries served in paper cones, little mason jars holding mashed potatoes, and potato skins in ramekins. To these my guests had the option of adding assorted condiments: chives, bacon bits, crème fraîche, butter, and truffle flakes; cheddar, blue, and Parmesan cheese; salt and pepper.

Try a mini sandwich bar or a taco bar. Just remember it's the colorful and varied condiments, how they are served, and how they are labeled that make the food station attractive and enticing.

No matter how delicious your food and drinks may be, don't worry. Your guests will save room for dessert. They always do. There must be merit to the "second stomach" theory. The good news is, your sugar-craving guests will not leave unfulfilled. I am famous for my dessert tables, and now you will be, too.

part six:

THE DESSERT TABLE

The dessert table should take your guests' breath away. There is no better way to dazzle your guests with drama, color, and the promise of mouth-watering deliciousness. The bite-size morsels, the saturated pastels, the smell of chocolate . . . When it comes to the dessert table, you must go all out.

Candy from CandyWarehouse: www.candywarehouse.com

The dessert table is the cornerstone of my parties. It is displayed throughout the event, so people can appreciate it with awe and wonder the entire time. What I love about the dessert table is that it awakens our inner child and reminds us of that excitement we used to feel when the cake arrived at a birthday party. Part of childhood is innocence—being delighted by something so simple as a sweet—and rediscovering that thrill brings about a spirit of true celebration. For one anniversary party that I planned, the couple was very fit and seemed to be watching what they ate at all times. But when it came to their party, all the husband could talk about was how he was going to be at the dessert table all night long. That is how fabulous your dessert table should be. It must be splendid enough to be an excuse for people to indulge, to break the rules, to let go. After all, isn't that the purpose of a party? And that is what the dessert table represents: the chance to free yourself, to enjoy the moment, to appreciate life.

my nanny's famous wine cake

1 box yellow cake mix (mix only)

1 3-ounce box instant pudding

3 eggs

1 teaspoon mace

¾ cup oil

¾ cup white Zinfandel wine or Riesling (You can substitute Kahlúa or dark rum to make rum cake. Or be creative and experiment with liqueurs. Rum and eggnog during the holidays make a fabulous, festive cake.)

1. Mix all the ingredients and put in a greased or sprayed Bundt cake pan.

2. Bake at 350° for 45 minutes.

3. When cool, you can add powdered sugar to decorate the top.

4. Okay, it's a cake, not a mini, but feel free to use mini Bundt pans. It's easy, and a guaranteed crowd-pleaser! So moist!

SUGAR

You can't go wrong with sugar. From simple chocolate chip cookies to mini soufflés, sugar is the great democratizer. Everyone loves it, and even if they don't love it, they can appreciate the beauty of a gorgeously presented confection.

I make sugar cookies for every single party. You can find cookie cutters to accompany any concept in the world. When you ice the cookies to match your color scheme, suddenly you have a beautiful, inexpensive, color-coordinated, yummy dessert that will be on display through most of the party.

Best of all, making cookies is hands down the most kid-friendly element of party planning. Stella, at age two, loves to use a squeezable pen to decorate cookies with glitter gel. Or she'll squeeze icing through the corner of a Ziploc bag, then stick tiny flower sprinkles or M&M's into it. Liam, on the other hand, is not as captivated by the delicate aspects of decorating. He likes to mix, bake, and eat.

I know there is a lot of support for cake and pie out there, but unless there is a truly compelling reason (like a birthday) I stick to bite-size desserts and here's why. People never cut into a cake themselves. It just sits there until the end of the party. Like my beautiful untouched Jell-O mold. Sigh. And if you do the cutting yourself, well, the minute you make the first cut into a cake, whatever decoration you've made is destroyed. It never cuts cleanly, and instead of looking like an elegant orchestra of color and design, the dessert table is instantly transformed into a desiccated mess.

People want to pick a small treat and try it. They may want to taste all the desserts. Why shouldn't they? Nobody wants six slices of pie, but what a delight to sample six minis! Anything can be done tiny. Cake pops, mini cakes, mini pies, mini cupcakes, mini ice-cream cones.

(continued on page 133)

{cutting the cake}
A TIP FROM CANDY

Hansen's is the most famous custom cake maker in Los Angeles. They made all my elaborate cakes when I was a little girl. Stella's second birthday party was a princess party. I wanted to get her a Barbie cake. I was remembering those cakes from the seventies, where a Barbie torso sat atop a semi-sphere of cake. Hansen's told me that they made them, but that the cake would be quite small. I don't like a small cake. If I have a cake idea that I like (and I always do) I want the final product to stand out. Of course it makes no sense when it comes to budget and waste, but the bigger the better.

For Stella's party we were only expecting fifteen to twenty people, but I wondered if there was a way to make the cake bigger. Hansen's is not to be defeated. They told me that they would find a bigger Barbie, and that they would make a cake skirt to fit it. They asked me if I needed to approve it, and I said no, that whatever they came up with was fine with me. (I should clarify that Hansen's was giving us this cake. If I'd been paying for it out of my own pocket, it would have been a different story.)

When the cake arrived, I was stunned to see the Barbie they had found. She was three feet tall—taller than the birthday girl! Where the skirt of her dress would have begun, there was cake. A massive cake. A cake that could have served three hundred people. Who knows what they used as a mold—a circular bathtub? Or did they have an ongoing demand for child-size Barbie cakes? I knew that cake would have cost thousands of dollars if I'd had to pay. It was spectacular.

When the moment came to cut the cake, I had to put Stella up on a table so she could reach it. I was aiming to cut the top of the cake, but at that moment my mother stepped forward to whisper in my ear, "That's going to come tumbling down. Always cut into the middle layer." Of course I deferred to my mother's years of party-hosting wisdom, and her technique was brilliant. I was able to cut perfect, portion-size pieces. When it comes to party planning, I always listen to Candy.

(continued from page 129)

Minis are more time-consuming because you have to decorate each little one. It's detail work, which I like. And remember, cookies can be done several days in advance. But if you're impatient with the fine art of cookie design, you can keep it simple and elegant: coat each cookie with a single color of frosting, then dust with a pinch of coordinating sugar sprinkles. Beautiful.

THE WOW FACTOR

Go crazy with color and theme at your dessert table. You must have many different desserts, and they must be displayed at all different heights. To create a range of desserts, look for something fruity, something chocolatey, and something sugary. Don't be shy with the food dye. Any non-chocolate dessert can be transformed to match your party, and almost anything can

be iced or embellished with icing. Use candy for dramatic color accents. As I learned from my mother, candy looks beautiful in tall glass jars.

You can achieve varying heights by balancing tiered cake plates with low trays, but you can also create levels on the table itself. For my back-to-school party, I put my dessert plates on top of stacks of books. You can also hide the books or sturdy boxes underneath the cloth—my kids' plastic toy bins, turned upside down, work perfectly. Look for other stackables that tie into your theme. For a Valentine's party, use piles of cheap heart-shaped chocolate boxes to create varying heights. For a tea party, vintage floral cookie tins, mismatched like your teacups, fit right in. Even the table can be thematic—I used an antique dresser for a shabby chic party, pulling open some of the drawers so I could display the trays inside, and I used a chalkboard table for my back-to-school party.

It's always a good option to rediscover a table that is already in your space. Clean off the top (for the first time in who knows how long), dress it with great dishes, and put desserts on that.

Choose the location of your dessert table carefully. If you shove it against a closet door, it doesn't have the magic. If it's the first thing people see when they enter, good luck steering them to the main food table. Put fabric or art behind the table to create a setting. A backdrop is definitely more work, but if you get a big blank canvas, you can do something as simple as painting stripes of color on it, or painting it a solid color with the guest of honor's name written on it in cursive.

I learned another tip from my mother about the dessert table at Stella's princess party. Because I had no idea that the Barbie cake we ordered was going to be gigantic, I had ordered "cake push-ups," which are like the push-ups we used to get from the ice-cream man, but instead of ice cream there was cake inside with frosting on top. You push the cake up as you eat.

I bought twenty of them, a little more than one per guest. To display them, I painted a square tin pink, which looked cute, then I put hot pink sand in the tin and stuck the push-ups in the sand to stand them up.

In the middle of the party, my mother rushed up to me and said, "Oh my God, you have no idea what just happened to me. I saw the cake push-ups standing on the table, and I assumed they were being held up by pink sugar, so I put a pinch of it in my mouth and it was *sand*."

I gasped in horror.

She went on, "You can't put sand in there! It's a dessert table. No, no, no. If you're making a display with sweets, people will assume it's edible." I use colored sand to hold lots of things up—signs, place cards, lollipops—but ever since then I make sure to use colored sugar on the dessert table.

Once your beautiful desserts are planned, it is time to put everything together and make the party come to life. The big day is upon you, but try not to freak out as much as I do. I'm here to walk you through it.

tori's red velvet cupcakes

INGREDIENTS FOR CUPCAKES:

½ cup butter, softened

1½ cups sugar

2 eggs

2½ tablespoons cocoa powder

2 ounces red food coloring

2½ cups all-purpose flour

1 teaspoon salt

2 teaspoons vanilla extract

1 cup buttermilk

2 ounces water

1 teaspoon white vinegar

1 teaspoon baking soda

INGREDIENTS FOR CREAM CHEESE
FROSTING:

1 8-ounce package cream cheese

½ cup unsalted butter

1½ cups powdered sugar

1 teaspoon vanilla extract

MAKE CUPCAKES:

1. Preheat oven to 350°.

2. Grease cupcake pan or line with paper liners.

3. Cream softened butter and sugar together until fluffy.

4. Add eggs and blend well.

5. In separate bowl, combine cocoa and food coloring and stir. When you have a thick paste, add butter/sugar mixture.

6. Sift flour and salt together into mixture.

7. Add vanilla, buttermilk, and water to mixture.

8. In another bowl combine vinegar and baking soda. Then fold into cupcake mixture.

9. Pour or spoon mixture into cupcake cups.

10. Bake 15 to 20 minutes or until a wood toothpick inserted into the middle of the cupcake comes out clean.

11. Let cool for about 10 minutes. Then put on a rack or plate and let finish cooling.

MAKE FROSTING:

1. Blend together softened cream cheese and softened butter.

2. Add powdered sugar and vanilla extract.

3. Blend until smooth.

4. Frost cupcakes and enjoy!

part seven:

FINISHING

TOUCHES

As the day of the party approaches, I am a roller coaster of emotions. Sometimes I have exciting breakthroughs, and sometimes I am bogged down in list-making. My favorite part is coming up with the elements of the party, but brainstorming can't go on forever. At some point I have to focus on bringing it all together.

Before I talk more specifically about the day before and the day of the party, let's cover a few key bases that put the finishing touches on your event.

music

Remember the days of the mix tape, monitoring your stereo while waiting for it to dub, accepting as standard the gaps between songs and poor sound quality, proudly labeling your cassette, and enjoying it for about a year before it got caught in the player, tangled, and ruined? Even if you are young enough to have avoided those times, you should thank God for digitized music. I'm not a music person. But as we all know, there must be music at parties. Some parties—particularly if you're evoking a certain era—call out for a certain kind of music. If you're as musically ignorant as I am, get a trusted friend to assemble a playlist for you. Making a playlist is easy and fun for those who, well, know what they're doing. Just try to come up with a song or two to give them a sense of the vibe you want. Even if you are having an elegant affair, the music should start out lively to get people excited and talking. As the party winds down, the music should shift to a more mellow vibe.

As hostess, you control the volume. Even if you love a full-on dance floor, make sure that if some of your guests aren't rocking out, they have a place to gather and talk. If the party is in a confined space, know that loud dance music will definitely alienate the wallflowers.

It is perfectly acceptable for you as the host to break out a signature dance move. I know this because at every event there comes a time when I must do the robot. Anyone who knows me can sense it coming, and as mechanical as it may look, it's the sign that I've finally relaxed.

entertainment

While I generally only bring in entertainment for my kids' birthday parties, you can enliven your party by finding small ways to spark conversation. It's nice to give people something to do. Sure, they're adults. They should be able to take responsibility for their own good time, but it doesn't hurt to give them a hand.

PHOTO BOOTH

My favorite bonus feature at a party is a photo booth. It is always, without fail, a big hit. When I say photo booth, I don't mean that you're literally bringing in a full-on photo booth. Instead, set up a little corner that forms a nice backdrop. Maybe there's a chair in front of a painting. If you're having a tropical party, drag a leafy houseplant into the frame and drape a South Pacific-y cloth over the wall. Or simply take an extra tablecloth that matches your party and tuck it around a chair. Set up a little bin of props. I like to provide old vintage picture frames that guests can hold around their heads, or chalkboards that they can write on and hold up in the picture. Put an old Polaroid camera out, and take a few pictures of yourself to show them how it's done. Who knows why, but people just love to take pictures of themselves at parties. And it gives them a nice souvenir to bring home. If you want to turn the photos into a favor, buy or make cute frames that can be put to immediate use.

CONVERSATION STARTERS

Use your party theme to get your guests thinking and talking. When Dean and I had our post-wedding wedding celebration, we put out little frames with

trivia questions about us like, "Where did Tori and Dean first say 'I love you'?" or "Why do Tori and Dean call each other 'babe'?" We put the answers on the backs of the frames. You can do the same for a guest of honor, or on the topic of a particular holiday. You can also ask more open-ended questions. For a wintertime "dreaming of summer" party you could ask questions like, "If you could go anywhere on a plane today, where would you go?" or "What is your favorite season and why?" Think of creative ways to display the cards. At a dinner party they can be at each place setting. Or to work the vertical space of your party, put them on pretty, colored cards, clothespin them to a string, and hang them above a serving table.

OTHER ACTIVITIES

Use the theme and setting of your party to inspire an interactive element. If the backyard is full of fireflies, you will of course provide beautifully labeled mason jars with holes punched in the top for firefly-catching. (You might want to have candles on hand for guests to add to their jars as they leave if they haven't managed to catch any fireflies.)

If there is a guest of honor, it's lovely to find a way for guests to make something for them in the course of the party. I am particularly fond of wish trees, where each person writes a wish for the person, couple, or family on a leaf-shaped tag and hangs it on the branches of the tree. The guest of honor goes home with a memento from every guest. I've also done group paintings, where I got a huge canvas and provided three or four jars of paint in the main colors of the party. Each guest had a chance to add a few strokes of paint to the canvas, and the result was a beautiful (well, I guess that's debatable) piece of art for the guests of honor.

For the Guncles' baby shower, they picked owls as a motif for their new baby girl, Simone. We bought ceramic tiles at "Color Me Mine," one of those stores where you glaze pottery and they bake it for you. All the guests painted owls and signed their names on tiles. After the party, I had the tiles made into a table for Bill and Scout.

As with food, I often draw inspiration from kids' parties. Musical chairs takes on a different tone when played by well-heeled adults, as does Twister. And everybody loves a piñata, especially if what's inside comes as a surprise. (Poker chips with numbers that correspond to real prizes, lip glosses for a girls' party, firecrackers at a Fourth of July party, even condoms or jokey sex toys. Just don't fill the piñata with wasps. Nobody likes that.)

WISH TREE
{how-to}

1. Find a nice tree branch about two feet tall.

2. Stick the branch into a box the size of a milk crate that is covered in fabric or painted.

3. Spray paint the branch white or silver.

4. Make a number of blank tags, with holes punched in them and ribbon tied through the holes.

5. Put out the tree, with the blank tags in a nearby bowl. Don't forget several pens.

6. Make a sign asking guests to write a wish on the tag and hang it on the tree.

pulling it off

Although I could happily plan a party forever, at some point I have to sit down, figure out everything that I have to buy, and write it all out. An organized person might love that. Not me. I do love going to the market, but I feel overwhelmed when I get home with all the paper products, ingredients, and craft supplies. I bring everything in from the car and then just stare at the bags. Now what?

I pull myself together, unpack a few bags, stare some more, draw a blank. Almost without fail, I proceed to have a panic attack. *Oh my God, I can't pull this off.* But eventually I manage to group my purchases into projects, and that makes it easier to face. As I start making stuff I get excited again. Designing the prototype of an hors d'oeuvre or a cookie is always fun. Then, halfway in, I flail again, thinking, *Oh my God, I have to make fifty more of these.* At that point I inevitably recruit Dean, who always patiently sits down to help. I give him the design model—a perfect example of what I'm trying to make—and he works from that. Now, Dean isn't as much of a perfectionist as I am. I've had to learn to relax a little. That swirl of cream cheese doesn't have to be perfect. (Or maybe I'll eat that one.) Eventually, with a little teamwork and a lot more patience than I have at my disposal, the job is done.

The day before the party, I want you to start from a clean base. Your home should be clean. Any furniture moving should be done (preferably with the help of several strong, shirtless men). All that's left is the fun stuff—and it should be fun (mostly) because otherwise, what's the point?

Do not spend the day before your party setting it up all by yourself. Haven't you and your friends spent enough time going out for lunch, or dinner, or drinks? Sell party prepping together to your friends as an opportunity to change things up. Promise cocktails and music. You'll chat, banter, and taste test while accomplishing a relatively simple task. If you want to matchmake, invite the would-be couple. They'll each want to show off how helpful and pleasant they can be. (Unless the setup is an instant success and they're too busy flirting to help, in which case you'll have to call in for backup.) The first thing you'll do this morning is make a run to the grocery store, so while you're doing that try to put a couple people on last-minute cleanup work or making favor bags so that while you're out, something is getting accomplished.

Time management on the day before the party is critical. Keep things moving. Don't get hung up scrubbing the grout in the bathroom for three hours. If a new dish isn't working out, scrap it and replace it with something familiar, or call a friend and ask if he or she would be willing to bring a substitute.

{checklist for} THE DAY BEFORE

☐ Spot clean. (You should have cleaned everything last week when you moved furniture!)

☐ Finish all food and beverage shopping.

☐ Prepare cold foods.

☐ Make desserts.

☐ Place flowers in buckets so they stay fresh overnight.

☐ Place décor: lay tablecloths; set out serving pieces, dishes, and glassware; position vases, votives, and favors. Complete and place signage.

☐ Enlist help for tomorrow if you don't have it already.

☐ At the end of the day make a list for tomorrow.

If you can't take the day before the party off, you must be sure that you have already cleaned and implemented any tricky décor elements in advance. Especially signage. Signage is an art, and you must not do it under pressure. Do all your food shopping and as much food prep as possible the night before.

Finally, try to get a good night's sleep. You'll want to be at your best tomorrow. As for me, I'm always up all night making stuff. The most sleep I ever get is about five hours, and the next day I am fueled by adrenaline (and Lipton onion dip). Maybe this is why I don't enjoy my own parties as much as I like planning them. Note to self: Get some shut-eye next time.

the big day

There are always last-minute details to attend to, including those bothersome guests who can't seem to follow simple instructions. Both your closest friends and the most fringe invitees alike will call with questions: What should I wear? Can I bring my children? Where do you live again? One of the hardest questions to handle if the answer is "no" is when a guest asks if he can bring a friend or friends to your event. Dean and I got married alone in Fiji, but a month later we had a wedding party to celebrate with our friends. It was a buffet dinner at a nice restaurant. One of Dean's best friends called the day of the wedding party. He said that he had a business meeting right before the party and wasn't sure if he could make it, but that if he did come, he would have to bring two friends from the business meeting. Now, our party was not a sit-down dinner, but we were still paying per head. But cost wasn't the only factor. His behavior was just plain rude. He didn't exactly sound like he was coming to the party to show his love and support for Dean. So Dean just responded, "Then don't come." He did come after all. Alone. On time. Some people just need boundaries.

TIMELINE

Your timeline for today should look something like this:

12:00 P.M. Best friends arrive to help move any furniture, set up floral arrangements.

1:00 P.M. Set up furniture and linens, set out food vessels and serviceware.

2:00 P.M. Set out signage, favors, other décor elements.

3:00 P.M. Prep hot foods and finish any other foods.

5:00 P.M. Shower and dress.

6:45 P.M. Toss salad, heat hot foods, light candles.

7:00 P.M. Party.

It looks better than it is. I never end up with time to shower.

Of course, even worse than people who don't pay attention to the names on their invitation are people who don't bother to call and ask before they show up with extra people. Funny, in my twenties it was fine to show up at a party with a friend who wasn't invited. That was the social norm. But now that my friends and I are all grown up, it no longer feels appropriate. I would never "crash" a party. When I see a guest walk in with two friends, I can't help but think, *Why didn't you tell me?*

LEAVING TIME TO GET READY

When the hour of one of my parties arrives I should be dressed and ready, but, truth be told, I never am. As people walk in, I'm still in jeans and a T-shirt, moving furniture, tying bows on favors, or putting dishes out. I need everything to be perfect, but apparently that doesn't include me. The doorbell rings and I run upstairs to change. There's never time to do my hair and makeup. I throw on a cocktail dress and flats, hoping against hope that I've accidentally stumbled into a casual, easy elegance, but the truth is that I've worked all day. I'm most likely a trainwreck.

In my twenties, my friends always came to parties fashionably late, or more than fashionably late. Our evening parties started at nine but didn't get going until after ten. Nowadays, everybody comes on time. Exactly on time. If not early. Maybe this is because most of us have children. That babysitter walks in the door and the parents are out.

I also find that people leave early. Maybe this is an L.A. thing, but nobody ever stays past ten. I recommend having all the heavy lifting done two hours before the party is meant to start. Get showered and dressed, then spend the hour before the party putting the finishing touches on the food and presentation. It's fine to be garnishing trays when your guests arrive, but you absolutely cannot break a sweat.

My fantasy is that I host all of my parties wearing dramatic caftans in all different colors. Preferably with a turban. No matter the occasion—pool party, holiday, black-tie event, kids' party. I'm always trying to get back to those days where people really dressed for the night and entertained. Caftans are just the right balance of theatrical, over-the-top, and comfortable. It doesn't always manifest, but that is my vision. I have a Slim Aarons

have a JENNY

I love my gay husband Mehran, but he is no use at parties. Most of the time he hides in a corner, reading magazines. My best friend Jenny, on the other hand, takes care of me at parties. She's done it since my first wedding, when she cut up a lamb chop with a fork and fed me like a baby. Jenny knows that I won't take the time to enjoy myself, so she is constantly putting drinks in my hand.

Also, Jenny is the life of the party. She can have fun anywhere, and her spirit is contagious. There is only one Jenny, but everyone should have one. And if you have it in you, try to be a Jenny for *your* best friend.

photograph of a woman. She is out by her pool, decked out from head to toe. She is wearing a caftan, beautiful bangles, a cocktail ring, heels, and big sunglasses. Her hair is perfectly coiffed, and she is holding a martini.

When I saw that picture, my heart stopped. I'm sure the photo was posed, but still. It looked like this was what she was wearing on a casual Sunday afternoon. That's the life I want.

Maybe the maxi dress is the new caftan. I'm glad long dresses are back in—they have opened the door for me to actually wear the caftans of my fantasy. But the truth is that although I do have a few caftans in my closet, when party time rolls around I'm too frantic and exhausted to feel cool enough to pull one off. Instead I throw on the first clean, unwrinkled dress I see, grab a bright lipstick, and hope for the best.

LOCK UP WILD PETS AND CHILDREN

I have a few pets. You know. Dogs. Chickens. A goat. I realize that not everybody has quite the menagerie that I do, but as much as you adore your furry friends, there are plenty of people out there who would rather not have a strange animal shove its nose in their privates the minute they walk through the front door. You must lock 'em up.

Of course, there are exceptions to every rule. If you have a chick farm, it can add to the life of the party. My silky chicken, Coco, likes to walk around with the guests and she is always the hit of the party.

You must also see to your young children. You don't have to lock them up, of course, but you should have a plan for them. Who will make sure they are fed? Who will put them to bed? Your mind will be elsewhere, and having a plan will make the night flow more smoothly for your kids and your guests.

WELCOMING GUESTS

As the guests arrive, take a deep breath. You have been focused on food and décor, but now it's time to shift focus. Stop worrying about the details and slow down. Greet your guests warmly as they come in. Show them the bar, get them a drink, and make sure they have found someone else to talk to before you tend to another guest. I always make sure I say hi to everyone once, and then I try to come back around for slightly longer conversations.

It is your job as the host to try to make connections. No matter how unique and fabulous your party is, if your guest doesn't talk to a soul she probably won't have a great time. The more people branch out into new and unexpected conversations, the more memorable the night will be.

You can't work social magic, but you can be a conversation starter. If two guests are standing near each other, introduce them and mention a person, place, or interest they might have in common. If your imagination fails, use yourself as the point of commonality. Tell them both how you met them. Or steer them to one of the points of interest you've established at the party. Like your Jell-O mold. They might not eat it (sigh), but they still might have Jell-O mold memories over which they can bond.

YOUR OWN GOOD TIME

At my parties I am always a nervous wreck. All that bouncing around, trying to please everyone, can be very stressful. But something makes me want to do it again. And again. I'll tell you what it is. At each party I have a moment. I survey the party, appraising each of the spots I've arranged with such care. I see it happening. Guests tasting cocktails, food being enjoyed. And

{trainwreck}
LIAM'S SECOND BIRTHDAY PARTY

For Liam's second birthday party, the theme was cars. It was one of my blowout parties, at a soundstage in Hollywood. There were lots of activities for kids, from an interactive dance floor to a photo booth where the kids got to sit in a little car. There was even a Build-A-Bear station. Because the party was going to be filmed for our show, vendors had come out of the woodwork to donate their services and treats.

But the morning of the party, Liam woke up sick. At first he just seemed cranky, with the sniffles. We had a huge party planned. All our friends were coming. I figured he would take a nap and feel better. It never occurred to me that he might miss his own birthday party.

When I put Liam down for his nap, he slept and slept. Finally, forty-five minutes before the party was to begin I woke him up. Now he was sick as a dog, coughing, with a temperature of 103.5. What could we do? We had to pull the plug.

By the time we knew we wouldn't make it to the party, it was nearly time for it to start. There was no time to let anyone know. Besides, if I told people we weren't going, they might turn around and drive home. I wanted people to go! It was all set up. It was fabulous. Somebody had to enjoy it!

From what I heard people managed to have fun without us, but Jenny was pissed. She never goes to Hollywood, and she thought I should have tried to reach everybody beforehand. (I did text as many people as I could as they arrived.) Jenny and I fought for weeks over this. I still to this day don't understand her logic, but she's my best friend so I eventually had to let it go and apologize because she wasn't going to see it any other way. Honestly, I didn't have much time to think it through. My son had a high fever, and he's prone to seizures. Jenny was right that I wasn't really thinking about other people. Liam's birthday. Had to have it. Bummer. Jenny doesn't go to Hollywood.

{tori TIP... IF THERE'S A SUDDEN CHANGE OF PLANS, SEND AN EMAIL BLAST TO COVER YOUR ASS.

then, out of the corner of my eye, I might catch a glimpse of a guest noticing one of the smallest details that I worked so hard to achieve. It's all worth it for that moment. Mission accomplished.

THINGS GO WRONG

No party is perfect. No matter how much planning you've done, people fall, things break, wine spills. Hard as it may be, no matter what happens it is your role as host to pretend it doesn't matter in the least. No matter if a guest toppled a valuable china lamp that was the only memento you had from your beloved and now deceased grandmother. *It doesn't matter in the least.* At one party a friend came to hug me and spilled red wine down the back of my new canary yellow chiffon dress. I didn't even bother to change (although that wouldn't have been rude). I think of how sweet my mother was when Stella and Liam each broke tree ornaments at her Christmas party. I felt terrible, but she instantly put me at ease. Whatever the disaster, take care of it as swiftly and calmly as possible and reassure your guest that there was no harm done. But do try not to end up mopping the floor on your hands and knees. The hostess should remain upright. The hostess's husband, on the other hand, may assume any position. (Got that, Dean?)

*celebra*T O R I

aftermath

When the party is over, I hope you look around and have a feeling of exhausted elation. You did it! Scan the food table to see what was a hit and what was left untouched. Check out the dessert table—sneak one last bite of decadence before you begin the task of cleaning up. The bigger the mess, the more of a success your party was.

I never mind the cleanup. There is no rush, except the lure of my waiting bed. But there is no question that cleanup is best if your closest friends linger to help. Then you can rehash the party—what worked, what didn't, who exchanged phone numbers, what social goofs transpired. That's the point, after all, to connect people, to create memories, and to share those moments with the ones you love.

part eight:
THE PARTIES

Okay, now your inner party planner is awake and raring to go. But before I send you out into the world to make your own party magic, I want to invite you to four—that's right, *four*—parties. (This book has got to be the most unique and personal party invitation ever—although it was a little gauche of me to charge for it.) These are very different parties that anyone can throw and I'm going to walk you through every step of the process. You'll find out how each was conceived, planned, and pulled off, and, best of all, you'll get to learn from my mistakes!

cowboys and lace party

the inspiration

My Cowboys and Lace party came out of the simple desire to find a concept that I'd never done before. I love the rough, worn aesthetic of cowboys, the west, and the otherworldly beauty of the desert. But as I was making my mood board, all the images I picked—a cowboy boot, a bolo tie, a hay bale, a horseshoe, a hand-painted sign, an old tin star nailed onto a wall—almost blended into one another too much. I needed something to create a contrast in look and feel. Lace seemed like the perfect juxtaposition. It is soft, light, and detailed, but still not completely out of place in the world of the Old West.

invitations

My first instinct on the invitation was to nestle an old horseshoe in a burlap-lined box with a tag that gave the party details. But it just wasn't practical to send a horseshoe in the U.S. mail. Turns out wrought iron is pretty heavy. Then I thought about making a layered invite out of leather, lace, and paper on top. I ended up going with an invite on rustic paper nestled in lace.

Text within image 1:

Cowboys & Lace
Giddy up Partners
And head to
Godwin Ranch
5188 Godwin Road
29 Palms, CA 92277
On May 13th
4 to 7pm

Dress: Vintage Western
RSVP by May 6th
See Ya'll there!

food

Dipping into the Internet for inspiration, I came up with a long list of stick-to-your-ribs man food that would work at a cowboy party. My list started out like this:

Corn on the cob	Chili
BBQ pork sandwiches	Cactus as an ingredient
Baked beans in a tin with a sausage sticking out	Mac and cheese in mini skillets
Cornbread baked in something unique	An onion ring tower
	Ribs

That seemed like a lot of food for one party, so I picked my favorites. This was my narrowed-down list:

Franks and beans	Onion rings
Ribs	Mini cornbread loaves
Mac and cheese	

It was still a lot of food, but what can I say? That's the kind of girl I am.

drinks

Even though I don't love beer, I couldn't imagine a cowboy party without it. But the signature cocktails would be the focus of the drink table:

Peach margaritas in mason jars with straws

Spiked lemonade

Cactus sangria

Shots of homemade whiskey (Well, it wouldn't really be homemade, but I did everything I could to make it look like moonshine.)

dessert table

My cowboy fantasy had weathered men recovering from a long day of herding cattle around a campfire. And what dessert would suit a campfire better than s'mores? I packaged graham crackers, chocolate, and a jumbo marshmallow in a handy kit tied with twine. My guests could pick a stick to roast the marshmallow, then assemble their own s'mores treat.

Cowboys require some down-home country classics, so I also made mini peach cobblers and mini pecan pies, which was an easy one for me since I've made it a hundred times. I baked several kinds of traditional cookies, but gave them cowboy names. The oatmeal raisin cookies were Chuck Wagon Cookies, the chocolate chip cookies were Lost Trail Cookies, and the peanut butter cookies were Point Riders. To round out the dessert offerings I added chocolate-dipped marshmallows and star-shaped fudge.

mini pecan pies

2¼ cups small pecan halves

⅓ cup butter

1 cup packed brown sugar

¼ cup sugar

¼ teaspoon salt

3 eggs

½ cup light corn syrup

1 tablespoon vanilla extract

Flour, for rolling out dough

pastry dough

½ to 1 cup large pecan halves

1. Preheat oven to 350°.

2. Place 2 cups small pecan halves on a cookie sheet and toast for 8 to 12 minutes.

3. Shake pan one time during baking. Make sure they toast but don't burn. Let cool completely and then chop.

4. Melt butter in a medium saucepan. Remove from heat and mix in sugars and salt with a wire whisk until all combined. Beat in eggs and then beat in corn syrup and vanilla.

5. Place saucepan over low heat. Cook and stir constantly with wire whisk until mixture is hot and appears shiny—approximately 6 minutes.

6. Remove from heat. Stir in the now-cooled toasted pecans.

7. Sprinkle flour and roll out dough. Place mini pie tin upside down on rolled dough and with a knife trace a circle around it.

8. Lightly grease pie tins.

9. Take the circle of dough and place in pie tin. With fingers pinch all around to make a fluted crust.

10. Pour pecan mixture into pie crust. Place large pecan halves on top of filling to decorate.

11. Bake pies at 350° until center is set, but soft when touched and moves slightly when pies are gently jiggled (about 25 to 30 minutes).

12. Move to wire racks and let cool completely (about 30 minutes).

Lost Trail
Cookies

décor

The general décor of the party draws from the rustic feel of cowboy livin': burlap and old gingham, rustic signage, a fire circle with low seating made of tree stumps. Vintage lace pillows gave the stumps a surprising twist—I'm pretty sure nobody has ever put stumps and lace pillows together. I used reclaimed wood to make trays and attached horseshoes as handles.

I had the party outside where there was a firepit that was key because, as everyone knows, cowboys like to kick back by a roaring fire. If you don't have a fireplace, buying a firepit just for a party is probably a little over-the-top, but you can replicate the feel by clustering candles in rusty old tins and burning some wood-scented incense.

For the floral arrangements, I put cacti in vintage mason jars and wild daisies in rusted tins. Tumbleweeds and cacti added to the desert vibe.

activity

Playing horseshoes was a no-brainer— a light lawn game that even cowgirls in heels can play. I wanted live banjo music but settled for a banjo mix on my iPod. For a more ambitious activity, I added a belt-making bar. I supplied a selection of leather belts, a hole puncher (not the normal kind—a special leather puncher), and the tools to let my guests stamp the letters of their names (or any other word) onto their belts. (Scout took it upon himself to brand the words "Yee Haw" onto his belt.) To finish it off, everyone picked out a buckle for their belt. By the end of the party every dude's pants were snug on their hips.

favors

I couldn't be more excited about the favors. One of the first images that came to me as I was planning the party was the favors: little cacti in their own pots. Once I bought the cacti, I realized they looked like little bald men, so I gave each one a mini cowboy hat. Stuck in each pot was a little toothpick sign that said, "Thanks y'all."

the party

One of my pet peeves about parties today is that they are too casual. What I loved about my cowboy party was that instead of being casual by default, it actively embraced our casual culture. People were invited to be lazy. They knew they didn't have to be on good behavior. We were all on cowboy time. We hung out playing horseshoes. We mellowed by the fire. Everyone was really relaxed. And my guests, who seem to leave early, stayed late. It was a party that felt like it had no beginning and no end, like the open skies of the great frontier. Heigh ho, Silver!

a do-it-yourself spa brunch

the inspiration

I fantasize about getting away to a spa with my girlfriends, but being with my family always wins out, so instead I decided to bring the spa to my backyard. When I was brainstorming this party I thought about all my favorite elements of spas—the scents of herbs and flowers, the taste and colors of fresh fruit, the oils and soaps and scrubs that make you feel refreshed and renewed.

invitations

Since I was only having ten girlfriends to my spa party, I was willing to go all out with the invitations. I would even hand deliver them to their houses if it were easier than packaging whatever I came up with. I toyed with writing out the invitation on a wide emery board, but decided it would be illegible. Then I thought about sending each girl a bottle of nail polish with the invitation stuck on in place of a label. Ultimately I decided to put a small loofah in a box, with a soap resting on it and an invitation sticker on the soap. I sprinkled dried lavender into each box. It was gorgeous.

SHORTCUT

If you're looking for an easier invitation, I recommend sewing two pieces of cloth together into a sachet. Stuff the sachet with lavender, sew it closed, and cut the edges to give it a scalloped finish. Finally, punch a hole in the corner and attach the invitation with a small ribbon.

food

A spa party called for light food, but I didn't want anyone to go hungry. Tea sandwiches are a no-brainer for a daytime party. I wanted each sandwich on the menu to have a fruity or herbal element to tie it into the theme, and I came up with three sandwiches:

Goat cheese and watercress

Cucumber mint

Grilled asparagus, prosciutto, and
  citrus mascarpone

There had to be a salad too, of course, so I added an arugula salad with toasted hazelnuts, pomegranate seeds, and a lemon-Parmesan dressing. I probably should have stopped there, but I added banana bread and fruit tea. Yes, I already had a full dessert table planned, along with a drink menu. But I'm just not a good editor. Why waste a good idea? To compensate, I tried not to go over-board with quantity. It was more fun for me that way—I like to change it up instead of making the same sandwich again and again like a factory worker.

SPA MENU

SANDWICHES

Goat Cheese and Watercress

Cucumber Mint

Carrot Ginger

Grilled Asparagus,
Prosciutto and
Citrus Marscarpone

Banana Bread and Fruit Tea

Arugula Salad with
Lemon-Parmesian Dressing

Rose Sorbet
Lavender Pops

drinks

At a spa party, hydration is key. Even a spa party should include cocktails, and I wanted mine to be a mix of flowers and herbs in refreshing, pastel colors. I added elderberry to rose champagne to give it a floral hint. And I made a mint and basil martini for the ladies who like an afternoon martini. I also made a rosemary lemonade with lavender ice cubes and strawberry-basil sparkling water. I put the liquors in cut-glass carafes. The lemonade and sparkling water were in glass drink dispensers. It all looked almost as refreshing as it tasted.

dessert table

When it comes to desserts, the emphasis is on the *party*, not on the *spa*.
Even a spa party needs a decadent table of sugar madness.

    I started with some light, spa-appropriate treats. I made a delicate rose
sorbet, which I served in vintage silver-and-peach glasses. And I made chic
rectangular lavender sorbet pops. They came out a beautiful milky white
with bits of visible lavender. I displayed them on a silver plate of lavender,
next to a little bowl of dried lavender.

My friend and fellow mompreneur Jenny Keller, who runs a cookie business, came down from Seattle to help me with the spa party. I met Jenny
at one of my book signings. Friends of hers brought me tins of cookies that
Jenny had made for the whole family: ladybug cookies for Stella, monkeys
for Liam, motorcycles for Dean, and nail polishes and lipsticks for me. They
were absolutely beautiful.

When I got home I looked Jenny up on Twitter so I could thank her, and
we've stayed in touch ever since. Now Jenny often helps me with my dessert tables when I run out of time. She's the best.

For the spa party we made red velvet cake lollipops. The cake was
coated in colored chocolate, then dipped in sanding sugar. We served cupcakes iced with buttercream that made them look like a tray of pink hydrangeas, and sugar cookies as always. I wanted the cookies to be in spa-related
shapes, and Jenny, genius, discovered that a baby bib cookie cutter, turned
upside down, makes a perfect claw-foot bathtub. To make cookies shaped
like spa masks, she realized that we could turn a heart upside down and cut
off the point with a bowl. Like I said: genius.

Finally, to fill out the table, we made mini cupcakes with little pearly
sprinkles that looked like bath oil balls.

décor

A spa is all about comfort and natural soothing, so it made sense to create a comfortable retreat in my backyard. (Foot soaking, mud masque, and living rooms are a risky combination.) We are so used to sitting outside on hard metal furniture or cushions that have been through a bit too much weather and are of questionable cleanliness. Putting indoor furniture out on grass has an immediate, dramatic effect. I pulled a huge, comfortable sofa outside (okay, I had a little help), and big, comfortable chairs.

I wanted a sort of shabby chic feeling, so I mixed weathered white furniture with pink flowers in different shades and mismatched floral dishes. The surfaces had a mix of treats and spa items. I used wire baskets for the spa-themed cookies. There were pretty glass canisters with cotton balls, plates with pure white nail buffers, and an old urn with peeling white paint to display the nail polishes. And I put individual servings of the salad in white pots that I found at a garden store, with chopsticks sticking out.

I mixed herbs in the food and beverages and they were reflected on the tabletops. The tables were garnished with bowls of dried roses and lavender. I pulled pieces from my beloved milk glass collection for the flowers and dried florals. This party is a perfect opportunity to put together mismatched pieces from around your house (or the garage sales you've been frequenting at my behest). Collect watering cans, tins, glasses, old teacups, old silver tins. Assemble those vases you've accumulated around your house. Put a cluster of them together on a wooden table with flowers that pull them together and you'll be amazed at how deliberate and professional it looks.

The same vintage suitcases that I used for a Game Night party found new purpose here—where they seemed manly and old world at Game Night,

they also fit with the shabby element of the spa. Big, vintage suitcases that ordinarily sit in a neat stack in my hallway. Who knew they would come in so handy? The same went for old vintage scarves that I find for a dollar a piece in secondhand stores. They make great mismatched table runners. Gather what you have, or make a run to a thrift store and see what you can find.

Under a big, shady tree, I created a second, separate low-to-the-ground little area for the mud masque bar with a couple loungers. That's right, I said mud masque bar. More on that later. To spice up the loungers, I wrapped

my ordinary beige outdoor cushions in floral tablecloths, using duct tape to hold the fabric in place. My friends thought I'd had the cushions recovered for the party, and I let them continue to think so—why not? I spread picnic blankets nearby in case more than two guests were in that area at the same time, and I put a tray in the middle of the blankets with more flowers and food.

For signage I stuck with the rustic look, using old wooden frames for my menus, with the inside painted in chalkboard paint so I could write the menu out (and make any last-minute changes or easily erase any mistakes).

FLOWERS

Flowers, flowers, flowers! Flowers were key at this party. I put together tight, round clusters of a single type of flower. This is called pavé style. When I do it I work from the outside in, placing the flowers in smaller and smaller concentric circles as I go toward the middle. As I work inward, I set the flowers increasingly higher so they create an even dome shape. You'll find that the stems from the flowers on the outside angle toward the center and help support the higher ones toward the middle.

For the spa party, I made my arrangements in milk glass vases and simple glass vases. I used white china mums, pink hydrangeas, pink roses, pink and white ranunculus, and pink peonies. Though I stuck to a pink palette and pavé arrangements, this party would also do well with a range of pastels in loose, easy arrangements. (I claim to like such arrangements, but when push comes to shove I always end up with the same tight clusters.)

I distributed them on the tables and at the mud masque bar. About that . . .

activity

Spa products are actually quite easy to make, but let's be realistic. Getting dinner on the table is enough of a challenge for me and most of my friends. I knew that a little mud masque mixology would be fun and I liked the idea of

sending my guests home with their custom product! Plus, it was an excellent excuse to make beautiful labels. I put the sign for the bar in a distressed white frame, and then I set out all the yummy ingredients: rose oil, raw honey, lavender oil, rosemary, dried rose buds, basil oil, rosemary oil. At a garden store I found gorgeous wooden herb stakes for the rosemary, lavender, and mint, but you could easily make stakes yourself.

*celebra*TORI

As favors I put homemade scrub in labeled mason jars. I could have had them leave with just the mud masques that they made, but (since I'm a control freak) I wanted the favors to be neat, with a label, out for display during the party.

HOMEMADE BODY SCRUB
{how-to}

1. Choose a salt: sea salt, Epsom salt, kosher salt, or even table salt. Fill half of a small bowl with it.

2. Pour oil over the salt until it is saturated. Oils that work well include almond, coconut, grapeseed, safflower, and avocado, but there's no need to run out and buy a fancy oil. Any cooking oil you have in your kitchen will do the trick.

3. Add about a teaspoon of honey—but it's your scrub so feel free to play with measurements.

4. Sprinkle in your favorite dried herbs—I like lavender, rosemary, and crushed rose petals.

5. Mix the ingredients well.

6. Put in a mason jar, tie with a ribbon, and tag for gifting.

the party

My favorite part of the Spa Party was when we put a mud masque on my friend Michelle, who has an eleven-month-old baby. She was wearing her new white robe and flip-flops and drinking rose and elderberry champagne. Michelle said that it felt like the first break she'd had in a year, and I thought, *That's the point!* We are all busy moms with busy lives. The party was a perfect way to decompress.

When I first put out all that yummy food and the beautiful desserts, I had a moment of wishing that I'd invited more people. But I always invite too many people. In the course of the party I realized how nice it was that this was a more intimate gathering. I actually got to talk to everyone, and they got to talk to each other. It was perfect.

game night

the inspiration

At a flea market I found a beautiful vintage Bingo spinner that made me fantasize about hosting a Bingo night. I bought it and brought it home. It sat in a box for a long time, stuck in the idea phase. A Bingo party wasn't quite enough. The more I thought about it the more I liked the idea of having a party that was inspired by *all* the games I loved as a kid. I started my brainstorm by making a list of games.

Twister	Chess	Chinese Checkers (board could be a tray)
Clue	Checkers	
Connect Four	Cards	Life
Backgammon	Tic-Tac-Toe	Operation
Domino (cookies!)	Hangman	Roulette
Croquet	Ouija	Pick-up sticks
Horseshoes	Boggle	Barrel of Monkeys
Monopoly	Scrabble	Tiddledy Winks

With these games in my head, I looked online at vintage game boards and decided that I wanted the feel of the party to be a dark, clubby atmosphere, with ivory, black, and burgundy tones, and elements of antique gold or brass.

This party would be the opposite of girly. The flowers would be minimal. Instead the focus would be on signage, nostalgia, and finding ways to carry the fabulous design elements of games to the party décor.

invitations

At first I envisioned invitations that drew from my vintage Bingo set. The cards were so beautiful that I thought I could somehow replicate them for the invitations. But I figured we would be playing Bingo at the party, and when there are so many options I don't like to repeat elements in such a major way. Instead I decided to make the invitations from vintage tarot cards, which are beautiful in their own right. I found mine on eBay. For each invitation I made an invite out of card stock the same size as the tarot card. With a gold grommet, I attached the invitation behind the tarot card so it fanned out when the guest opened it.

GAME NIGHT

Come play by the rules
2.12
7-10 o'clock
DRINK, EAT, AND WIN!
Dress: your best game face
Tori's House

The food for Game Night had to be old-school American food that belonged in a smoky club. I knew exactly what I wanted:

Sliders

Mini club sandwiches

Little veggie and chicken potpies

Meatloaf

Chips and dip

In the weeks leading up to the party I gathered a bunch of props. Many of them were simply old game boards, but in my flea market and tag sale wanderings I also collected anything that had the same feel and color scheme as the party: old bowling pins with burgundy bands around their necks, an hourglass, old leather suitcases, glassware with gold details, old wooden crates, ice buckets with backgammon designs on the outside, argyle socks (why not?), and, the best treasure of all, a beer jug in the form of a rather evil-looking clown.

I brought out all the food, put it on the designated food table, and started playing. I found trays for each food—a Chinese checkerboard for the mini meatloafs, a couple round brass trays for the sliders and potpies. I moved the bowling pins and hourglass around, trying to get a sense of how it all fit. But what was clear to me was that the table was too big. The food looked lost. So I pulled out a big leather suitcase and put it right in the center of the table, flush against the wall. With the suitcases and some old books creating levels, suddenly the table looked less crowded.

I kept playing, bringing in a small silver votive with a single dark red dahlia, then taking it away, switching the bowling pins from left to right, shifting the suitcases and swapping in different florals—a tight bunch of dark red carnations. A vintage checkerboard leaned up against the wall made a perfect backing. The club sandwiches went on a Scrabble board, which made an excellent tray. They were held together with glass toothpicks, but for some reason, maybe it was the Scrabble board, they just looked like plastic. So I switched the toothpicks to regular wood ones with a little red crinkle ribbon at the top. I had some mini sliders on a Parcheesi board that I really wanted to use. But as the whole table came together, I could see that those sandwiches just didn't look great, so, much as it pained me, I finally ditched the Parcheesi board. At last, the food table was perfect.

*celebra*TORI

drinks

I happen to own a mid-century punch bowl that I thought would look perfect at the party. The punch was less important than the bowl. It's a perfect example of how I let what I have on hand drive some of the party elements. I made Scrabble Sangria. The red sangria looked beautiful in the bowl.

PUNCH

I knew I wanted to use Boggle cubes as a decorative element, and what better way to do so than to freeze them in ice cubes. (Never do this if small children are likely to suck on the ice cubes!) Presto—a chilled Boggle Bellini.

For my second cocktail I made a Barrel of Monkeys Martini—again, a variation on a martini, but this one had a little red monkey from the game Barrel of Monkeys dangling over the edge of the glass. Adorable.

I had two galvanized tin tubs for drinks, but when I unloaded brightly colored Jones sodas in them, it all looked too bright and perky for the muted, masculine tones of the party. I moved the bottles to a wooden crate that was divided into squares, where the bottles nestled perfectly. The rustic, faded wood created a perfect contrast with the colorful bottles.

dessert table

I love a candy table, and Game Night was a perfect excuse to pick some of
the most visually appealing vintage candies and display them. Because who
doesn't like to nibble candy while playing games? I looked for candies with
colors and fonts that felt more muted and old world.

In big glass jars with rusted lids I put massive quantities of Mary Jane candy, gummy soda bottles, lollipops shaped like dice, circus peanuts, red licorice, brown wax mustaches, and red wax lips. It was inexpensive, and the results were stunning.

On the candy table I set out white paper bags, each stamped with the image of a game card, so people could fill a bag with assorted candy and bring it back to the game they were playing.

Just because I did a candy table didn't mean I was going to skimp on dessert. *Au contraire.* I turned a huge old red steamer trunk on its side to make a table—a wooden crate would have the same effect. On the surface I created an artistic masterpiece, balancing real games with the game desserts. There was a box of real dominos, a Magic 8 Ball, and, on top of a stack of vintage games, the vintage Bingo spinner that inspired the whole party.

Surrounding the vintage ephemera were the desserts. There were cupcakes, of course, each one with a different scrabble tile cookie. Balanced against the real dominos were cookies decorated to look like dominos. And near the Bingo spinner were white Bingo ball cake lollipops and sugar cookies iced to look like Bingo cards. To fill out the table, I made mini cupcakes—chocolate with white icing and red candy on top.

Dice Lollipop

décor

I knew from the very start that I wanted to make my living room feel like an old library. If I knew how to replicate the scent of mildewing books I would have done it! But I had to settle for borrowing the oldest, most leathery furniture I could find. I scouted at yard sales for anything that was brown, ivory, burgundy, and antiqued gold. Some of my finds were on the extravagant side—like the chess table. (Dean just shook his head when he saw that one.) But some of my favorite items were so inexpensive that I felt okay knowing I might only use them for this party, like the old clear bottles that I clustered on the mantel.

For an economical centerpiece, I filled a big oval wooden tray with Cracker Jack boxes. When I discovered that I didn't have enough boxes to adequately fill the tray, I looked around for something to fill up the bottom of the tray so I could stack them higher. I settled on some old books, which would still look nice even as people removed boxes and exposed them.

As I said, I knew going into this party that the flowers wouldn't be fussy. For vases I used tarnished silver flea market finds. You could also use simple glass vases or regular drinking glasses. We didn't need many flowers, but I prepared a few single-stem dark red dahlias in tarnished silver votives, and clusters of dark red carnations in other miscellaneous containers. I always make up the flowers without knowing where they're going to go. Then, as I set up the food, dessert, and side tables, I tried the flowers out in different conformations until I was happy.

I planned for us to sit around the fire playing games, so I clustered everything brass or gold in the house on the mantel: random trophies, old bottles, and one or two brass stags (an eBay score). I took some brown-and-plaid blankets, rolled them up, and put them in a basket in front of the fire. I just did this because I happened to have the blankets and I wanted to exaggerate the feeling of warmth that the fire generated. And when I saw argyle socks in a sale bin at the store, I couldn't resist. I loved the idea that people would cozy up by the fire to play games, taking off their shoes and slipping on some of the nice warm socks that I would display in a wicker basket. (Besides, Dean needed some new socks anyway.)

I stripped the couches of their regular throw pillows and brought in huge, overstuffed pillows that I had made to look like game cards and dice. I figured as the night went on, some of the games might require people to sit around the table, and I wanted people to pull down the huge cushions and sit on them as needed. The big white pillows were cute, but for all my efforts, once I put them out in the room I saw that they looked way too bright and had to scrap them. It was painful, but it's important to be able to admit when something that you worked on doesn't come out right. Don't display your mistakes just to convince yourself you didn't waste time.

I looked around the room to find the perfect places for the rest of my props that hadn't found homes. The vintage poker chips went on the food table. The playing card coasters went on the central game table, so the players would have some place for their drinks.

LEATHER TABLE
{how-to}

1. Find a cheap antique coffee table or side table—an easy score at local yard sales or flea markets. It can be scuffed or beaten-up because you'll be covering the top.

2. Take a large piece of leather and drape it over the top of the table.

3. Flip the table upside down and cut the leather so it extends a couple inches beyond the perimeter of the table.

4. Use a staple gun to staple the leather under the table. Make sure you keep the leather pulled tightly as you do this so you don't have any ripples in the leather.

5. Voilà! A leather-top table.

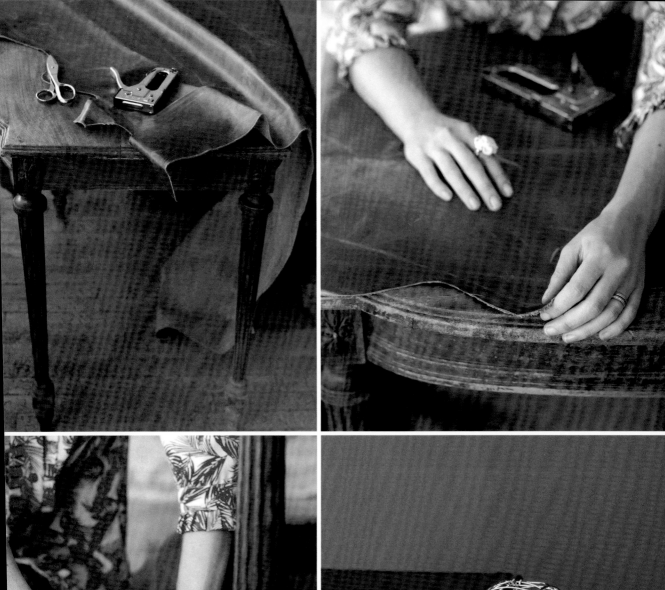

activity

When I was looking over the list of games I loved as a kid, I got stuck on Clue. The board game, a whodunit where you try to figure out who murdered the fictional Mr. Boddy, had a great setting—a manor complete with a billiards room and secret passageways. The characters had excellent names and colors—Miss Scarlett, Colonel Mustard, Professor Plum; their weapons were so retro-fabulous— the candlestick, the revolver, a lead pipe! I got momentarily obsessed with switching over to a murder mystery party where all the guests would come dressed as characters from Clue. But instead I settled on setting up a Clue photo op, with props and costume elements from the game that people could use to pose for Polaroids. A pipe, a rope, a candlestick, a mustache, a velvet jacket. I hung the props on Dean's coat rack and set out some picture frames the guests could hold around their faces to add a little whimsy. Perfect!

Of course the central activity of the evening was a variety of games. I put several out to give my guests options (fantasies of coed naked Twister), and on an easel near the fireplace I set up a game of Hangman, which I knew would be an easy, no-pressure game to rev up my sometimes apathetic friends and start the ball rolling.

favors

For my favors, I found little leather drawstring bags. I put a pair of vintage dice (I know, I know—I always take it a little too far) in each bag and made a tag that said, "Thanks for rolling with us!"

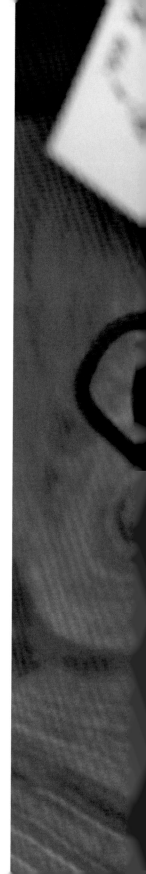

the party

I managed to make it to Game Night fully dressed and ready to play. I wore a gold-and-black vintage YSL blouse with full sleeves and a bow at the neck. Like a true master of ceremonies, I was still sliding around tables as the guests arrived.

There was some initial resistance to the games. Bill and Scout both said that this would be the first time they had played games since age ten. But they couldn't protest too much. It's not like I was asking them to write essays about how they spent their summer vacation! Games are fun.

We played Scrabble and Hangman. Stella was asleep, but Liam came in and joined Scout and Bill's Scrabble team. I'd like to say that they were unbeatable, but, well, it just wouldn't be true.

Eventually, after a slider and a taste of mini meatloaf, I joined the games. Later, when I looked at the pictures of that night, I saw one of me playing Scrabble and thought, "That's the life I want!" I was relaxed and happy, holding a martini, with all my gays around me. It's a rare moment when I actually feel so happy with a party that I'm actually in the party, sharing the moment, living it. That special and awesome feeling is what was captured in that picture.

cocktails
in caftans

the inspiration

I love the work of the American photographer Slim Aarons, who took pictures of the rich and famous living lives of exquisite leisure. I have some of his photographs, and they show well-heeled women drinking decadent cocktails poolside in Palm Springs. Slim Aarons, along with my longtime fantasy of wearing a caftan to host a party, inspired my Cocktails in Caftans party.

For a color palette, I looked through my book of Pucci images. I wanted a seventies feel, but nothing too psychedelic or outrageous. Also, since the party was going to be outside, I wanted colors that would pop against my tropical green setting. I settled on muted oranges that graduated toward brown and yellow.

I made a mood board, pulling images of poolside glamour, agate coasters, a cigarette balanced in a mod glass ashtray, even a shot of Mr. and Mrs. Roper from *Three's Company*. By the time I was done, I couldn't wait to be at the party.

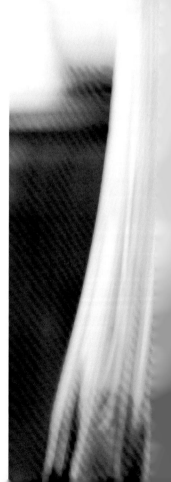

invitations

When I tried to think about iconic images or items from the early seventies that might lead to an invitation idea, I couldn't get much beyond cigarette holders and paperweights. Remember, I didn't want to go the hippie route. Finally, I came back to my original inspiration—the resort-chic caftan. In

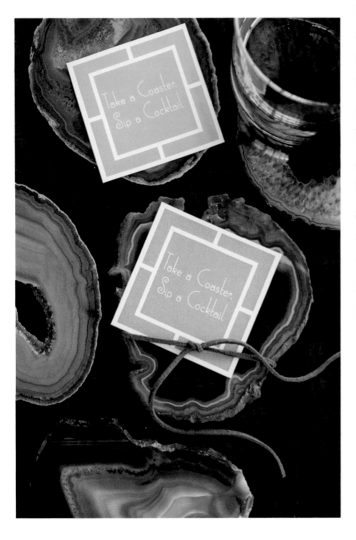

the scarf bin of my local thrift shop I looked for the most seventies-style fabrics I could find. For the invitation everyone got a scarf, tagged as if it were on sale, but instead of the price, the tag gave the party details. I liked the idea that people (well, the female guests at least) could use the scarves for their hair or to tie on their purses. I put a tortoiseshell napkin ring around each scarf, and sent it in a box.

food

At a chic party like this I wanted my guests to feel fancy and pampered. We would have to have passed trays of hors d'oeuvres. I used the same trays I use for every party, but this time I sprayed them with a high-shine lacquer so they were sleek and elegant. For the food, however, I went more retro-kitsch. There was cheese fondue, mini quiche Lorraines, deviled eggs, Swedish meatballs on furry-topped toothpicks, and mini iceberg lettuce wedges with homemade bacon bits and green goddess dressing served on wooden plates. And we had to add crab rangoon, a dish that I fell in love with at Trader Vic's, where it is a staple on the menu.

drinks

I knew exactly what cocktails I wanted to serve. As a salute to my mother,
I had to serve whiskey sours. When I was growing up, whiskey sours were
my mother's drink. In the same way a girl's first perfume is what her mom
wears, when I turned twenty-one I made the whiskey sour my drink. At
bars my friends would order beers or wine coolers and I'd order a whiskey
sour. Then came the day I threw up whiskey sour all over the elevator at
the Manor. After that I wised up and switched to wine. So we had whiskey
sours, Harvey Wallbangers (an orange drink that looked great with our colors), and pineapple daiquiris in my favorite vintage punch bowl.

dessert table

In keeping with the kitschy food vibe, my dessert table had mini Jell-O molds, mini ladyfinger cakes, mini baked Alaska, and mini pineapple upside-down cakes. There was chocolate fondue with pineapple chunks, strawberries, angel food cake, and Rice Krispies Treats for dipping. My cookie-genius friend Jenny and I bought edible icing that looked like different kinds of marbled stones— malachite, agate, and tiger's-eye— and used it on top of sugar cookies. They were the most elegant cookies you've ever seen.

décor

As with most of my outdoor parties, I wanted to bring the comfort of indoors outside. In the case of this party, the décor was about rediscovering a sophistication that has been lost over the last few decades, and mixing it with the coziness of today.

Slip on a
Pair of
Shades

I knew it would be hard to do flowers for the caftan party. Flowers are organic. They tend to soften and prettify any environment. But I wanted a modern look. I wanted clean angles, simple and bold lines, hard edges. My choice was clear. I was going to make Lucite mum balls. There was nothing better for a clean, modern look, and they would be the main décor element of the party.

In addition to the mum balls, I served drinks using glassware in primary seventies colors: green, yellow, orange, and amber.

For this party in particular, the attire was important. It was actually part of the décor. I was relying on my guests to embrace the caftan theme and come decked out in resort chic. I knew getting glammed up like that would set their mood, and set the mood of the event. To help out a bit, I supplied some accessories. There was a glam ashtray filled with big cocktail rings and a sign that read, "Slip into a cocktail ring." On a big piece of driftwood I put out big, colorful bangles that guests could use to add to their looks. And as they walked through the doors to the back-yard, I displayed a supply of chic sunglasses they could put on before making their way out to the deck.

LUCITE MUM BALLS
{how-to}

Lucite mum balls are clear plastic boxes with flower balls inside them. They look expensive and amazing, but they are cheap and easy to make.

1. Buy Lucite boxes. I found mine at The Container Store. They come in all different sizes but I chose the size that's meant to showcase soccer balls. (I had a much better use in mind, though if I were having a sports party I suppose I might put a soccer ball on a nice bed of Astroturf as a decorative element.)

2. Soak several balls of floral foam (one for each box). The trick is to soak the foam in water until it is so drenched that it sinks to the bottom of its container without your help.

3. Pull stems apart from the mum bunch. Cut each stem, leaving 1 to 1½ inches of stem. (Carnations make great floral balls, too.)

4. When the foam is fully soaked, stick one color of mums or carnations into it until it is completely covered.

5. Set it in the box. That's it, done! The final product lasts about one or two days.

6. You can display the balls in many ways: with or without boxes, lined up, bookending a table, even stacked in towers or hanging (boxless, of course) by ribbons. Experiment!

activity

I wanted an interactive element for the party, but nothing too raucous or goofy since I wanted this party to stay cool and chic. I knew everyone would look glamorous, so I set up a Polaroid camera and a backdrop where they could take pictures of each other and document their fabulousness.

favors

For favors each guest received two agate slices that they could use as coasters at home. They were tied together with a ribbon and a little tag that said, "Take home a coaster. Sip a cocktail."

the party

The caftan party was really my pièce de résistance. I finally got to be that hostess that I'd dreamed of being, wearing the caftan, carrying the martini. While my Cowboys and Lace party was fun and relaxing, this party was something else. If the Cowboy party was close to who we are, the Caftan party was what we aspired to be (for a few hours, anyway). We took on the vibe of the party, and for a moment we were all transported to another time and place. It was unforgettable, and I hope yours is, too.

*celebra*TORI

{afterword}

the party's a wrap

When the lights are up, the music's off, and the party's over, I'm tired and victorious. After all that work, it's hard to believe it's over. And because a party is just a moment in time, all you have when it's done are the photos, any souvenirs your guests may have created, and the memories. But let's not underrate those memories. I love and revel in the design and details, and I definitely get caught up in the process, but when all is said and done what I want to give my guests, above all, is an unforgettable experience. When I'm old and gray (except you know I'll never let the gray happen), I know I'll look back at the photos of these parties with my same old friends and feel happy and proud that I created something fun and beautiful. The parties themselves may be short and ephemeral, but those memories will last forever. Thanks for sharing them with me.

{acknowledgments}

DEAN, LIAM, AND STELLA: Thank you for your love, support, encouragement, enthusiasm, and patience through the process of bringing to life this passion project of mine. I think I have two mini party planners on my hands—xoxo.

HATTIE: Thanks for enduring the crazy schedule of this book shoot while in my belly, and for giving me severe morning sickness throughout. Already a strategist like Mom! I love you.

GUERAN AND RUTHANNE: Thanks for being great agents and amazing friends. You always listen to my ideas and passionate babble and then make it a reality.

DAN STRONE: Thanks for helping me achieve another vision through the execution of this book.

JAMIE: Thanks for always going to bat for me and making my dreams come true. I consider you a true friend.

MY FRIENDS: Thank you for your constant support and for always coming to every party I throw even when you think it's a crazy theme.

MY FAMILY AT GALLERY BOOKS: Thanks for continuing to give my voice and ideas a home and for supporting all my passions and visions.

JAMES MCGOWAN: Thank you for being a true partner. We don't always see eye to eye, but it's our shared visions that make for such unique and exceptional events. I want to throw parties with you for the rest of my life! I love you.

CHRIS WROBLESKI: Thank you for your creativity, party passion, and for always offering to jump in to help me out. Especially when I have big ideas, a small budget, and no time . . . Always.

JESS TOHIR: Thank you for always going above and beyond and always with a smile on your face. You were such a great addition to our party-planning dream team. And I love your shaky man hands!

BRANDY SHARP: Thank you for always donating your time to help me out as a friend. You constantly have my back and remind me to believe in myself.

JENNY KELLER: Twitter connected us for work, but the love of the party made us friends. You inspire me on so many levels. I respect you as a mom, wife, friend, and exceptionally creative baker. You're the complete package, my friend! Now just move to L.A.!

JACLYNE BREAULT: We met doing weddings and I'm so happy you came into my life. Your creativity is endless and most of all you GET me! You understand my attention to detail because your attention to detail is flawless. We love our Jacs!

AMBER MOON: I had all the pieces to my party-planning skills mastered except tags . . . till I met you! You came in at the last minute on this book and saved the day. You execute my vision beautifully and then some. Thank you!

JENI MAUS: I love your style like no other! Thank you for always believing in me and my ventures and being so willing to jump on board to help me out. This book would not have been complete without you and your amazing pieces.

SARA REMINGTON: Sir Remington, you are one of a kind! I had such a distinct vision for this book but you completed that vision and then kicked it up five notches. You are beyond amazing and your energy is inspiring and mesmerizing. You made long, overwhelming days seem fun and effortless. I look forward to many ventures together.

DANA WASHINGTON: Thanks for organizing my life and allowing me to semi-manage fifty projects at once without going insane. It's a crazy life, but I'm glad you're along for the ride with me.

ELIZABETH MESSINA: My personal photo goddess. Thank you for letting me use the pictures from some of the most personal and magical events I've ever thrown that only you could capture the way you do.

HILARY LIFTIN: Doing a book without you wouldn't be a book at all. We are a true team at this point. I don't think there's any kind of book we couldn't do together. Through all of it you are my rock. And working in bed together during my first trimester of pregnancy when I was so sick took our relationship to a whole new level!

PATRICK PRICE: My extraordinary editor and friend. You know and get me so well. I love that you encourage my humor and appreciate all my quirks. I adore you and our relationship. You make my written word and vision the best it can be.

JUSTIN, AARON, AND KRISTIN: Thank you for all of your hard work. I know it was a job, but you went above and beyond as friends to help execute my visions. We all worked as a team and I couldn't have done it without you.

COCO: My party-planning muse. You kept all our spirits up during an impossible schedule. And, you're quite possibly the most photogenic chicken on earth.

{credits}

ART DIRECTOR . . . . James McGowan

PHOTOGRAPHER . . . . Sara Remington

DIGITAL TECH/FIRST ASSISTANT . . . . Shawn Corrigan

FOOD STYLIST . . . . Katie Christ

FOOD STYLIST FOR SPA PARTY . . . . Sienna DeGovia

ASSISTANT FOOD STYLIST . . . . Lillian Kang

EVENT AND PROP PRODUCER . . . . Jess Tohir

MAKEUP ARTIST . . . . Brandy Sharp

ART DEPARTMENT . . . . Justin Turner

ART DEPARTMENT . . . . Aaron Rand

ART DEPARTMENT . . . . Kristin Rasmussen

FLORALS . . . . . Jaclyne Breault/Heavenly Blooms, HeavenlyBlooms.com

FURNITURE AND PROPS . . Jeni Maus/Found Rentals, Vintage-rental.com

TAGS, INVITES, AND LABELS . . . . Amber Moon/Pitbulls and Posies,
Pitbullsandposies.com

DESSERT TABLES . . . . Jenny Keller/Jenny Cookies, Jennycookies.com

SEVENTIES HOUSE DESIGN . . . . David Houck, Houck Inc.

{about the author}

TORI SPELLING is an actress whose career spans theater, television, and film. She's received critical praise for her work in such independent films as *Trick* and *The House of Yes*. She and her husband, Dean McDermott, are the stars and executive producers of Oxygen's hit reality series *Tori & Dean: Home Sweet Hollywood*. The #1 *New York Times* bestselling author of *sTORI telling, Mommywood, uncharted terriTORI,* and *Presenting... Tallulah*, she lives with her family in Los Angeles.